ORCHIDS

ORCHIDS

Photographs PAUL STAROSTA
Text MICHEL PAUL

EVERGREEN

Above

Maxillaria ubatubana (×1)

The orchid

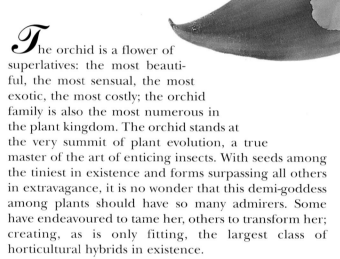

The orchid is a flower of superlatives: the most beautiful, the most sensual, the most exotic, the most costly; the orchid family is also the most numerous in the plant kingdom. The orchid stands at the very summit of plant evolution, a true master of the art of enticing insects. With seeds among the tiniest in existence and forms surpassing all others in extravagance, it is no wonder that this demi-goddess among plants should have so many admirers. Some have endeavoured to tame her, others to transform her; creating, as is only fitting, the largest class of horticultural hybrids in existence.

A numerous and astounding family

The 25,000 to 30,000 known species of orchid make up the family of the Orchidaceae, which (though this may not be apparent at first sight) are related to the Liliaceae (tulips, lilies, etc.). A typical characteristic of this family is the bilateral symmetry, as opposed to radial symmetry, of their flowers. This means that, if an imaginary line is drawn through the centre, the same features appear on either side of that line (as in a human being: one arm on each side, one eye on each side, and so on). In a daisy, on the other hand, the same features appear around a central point. Another special feature is that it is impossible to distinguish separate

pistil and stamens in an orchid flower. These are in fact fused into a single, cylindrical organ known as the column*. At the end of this central column is the stigma* and what remains of the stamens; these take the form of two pollen masses, each carried on a small stalk, the caudicle*, and are called pollinia*. The corolla has three petals, the middle one, known as the labellum*, being quite distinct from the other two in shape, colour and size. This highly original flower form is completed by three sepals which usually resemble petals in that they too are coloured; in most cases the three sepals are not identical.

Why such sophistication? Flowers, as we know, are designed to attract pollinators. So, since orchids are the most highly evolved flowers, the answer is fairly obvious: in this family, the relationship between insect and flower has been developed to perfection.

Orchid and insect in perfect harmony

Observing certain European orchids, such as Ophrys, from a short distance, one often has the impression that an insect is resting on the flower. A closer look reveals the truth: the colours, the shape and the hairiness of the labellum mimic an insect. This is how these plants have acquired their names – the bee orchid (*Ophrys apifera*), the bumblebee (*Ophrys bombyliflora*), wasp, fly, hornet ...

If man were the only creature to be taken in, it would be of no benefit to the flo-

Above

Lycaste aromatica (× 1.2)

wer, but the trap works well for insects too. The males of a certain type of insect recognize in a particular species of orchid a female of their own kind. The deception goes yet further, because the flower has the same scent as that of the female in question. The male loses no time: he swoops down and attempts to mate with what he believes to be a female. In doing so, he encounters the pollinia of the flower, held upright on the caudicle, ready to stick to his head or abdomen. Frustrated in his purpose, the male departs, bearing his cargo of pollen, in search of a fresh conquest. Some time later, he makes another attempt, adopting the same mating posture. In the meantime, the orchid has prepared itself for the second assault: the caudicles of the pollinia are curved over in such a way that the pollen masses are now positioned at the far front (of the head) or rear (of the abdomen), aligned with the sticky surface of the stigma so as to adhere easily. Had they remained vertical, as they were the first time, pollination could not have taken place. This is how self-pollination* is avoided.

The artifice can be refined still further. In some insects, the males emerge before the females. Their first thought on emergence is to ensure continuation of the species, but all they find are imitation females, resting serenely on their flowers and exuding their attractive scent. At this point, the orchid has no competitors.

Not all orchids stoop to deception. Like most flowers, many of the Orchidaceae are content to offer nectar and perfume...with the bonus of a broad landing site (the labellum) and elegant guidelines luring the insect to its reward (the nectar) and to its involuntary cargo (the pollinia).

In some species of orchid, if no insect visits the flower, the caudicles of the pollinia become dry and allow the pollen to come into contact with the stigma of the same flower. In this case, self-pollination takes place. In other species, this phenomenon occurs before the flower has had time to open, and occasionally, in some species, fertilization takes place while the plant is still below ground!

Orchids may have made a finer art of 'love' than any other flower, but their 'maternal instincts' are sadly lacking. Indeed, their offspring have little chance of growing at all.

From the flower of greatest complexity to the seed of greatest simplicity

Two or three days after pollination the flower fades and droops, unless it has been fertilized. If it has, the petals and sepals change colour and wilt but remain attached to the ovary, which lies behind the flower. This swells into a fruit, in the form of a capsule. On reaching maturity, which may take from five to fifteen months depending on the species, this splits open to release a dust made up of thousands, even hundreds of thousands, of seeds. These minute seeds are extremely light, and easily carried away on the slightest of breezes. However, they contain no food reserves, so they cannot germinate independently. For this, an orchid seed must be invaded by a fungus which supplies the necessary nutrients for germination and development. In certain cases, the fungus continues to grow in the roots of the adult plant. This is how one orchid without chlorophyll, *Neottia nidus-avis*, is

able to live, a genuine example of symbiosis. Although the seed can survive quite long, many wait in vain for the fungus to arrive. So, despite their enormous number, few orchid seeds grow into a new plant.

Even when all the necessary factors combine to ensure success, many years must pass, up to fifteen for some species, before the new plant is able to reproduce in its turn.

Variety in growth habit

An ultra-light seed can reach the tree-tops with no difficulty. For this reason, we find two types of orchid: terrestrial orchids, which, as the name suggests, grow on the ground, and epiphytes*, which establish themselves on trees.

Each type can grow in two different ways:
– the sympodial* orchids in which the new growth emerges alongside that of

Leaves, roots, rhizomes and other pseudobulbs

The great variety of modes of life and growth of orchids explains the impressive morphological* diversity of their organs.

the previous year, causing lateral spread, and – the monopodial* orchids whose new growth is added to the apex, increasing the plant's height.

Sympodial orchids

Roots grow downwards from the rhizome*, the short stem which develops below ground (terrestrial orchids) or on the support (epiphytic orchids), while stems and leaves grow upwards from it. Most epiphytic species, such as those of the genera* *Cattleya, Laelia, Brassavola, Odontoglossum, Ansellia* or *Dendrobium,* have storage organs in their stems, to help them withstand the dry season. Their shape varies from species to species but there is always a bulb-like swelling,

above

Encyclia prismatocarpa (×1.2)

hence the term pseudobulb*. The leaves appear at the extremity of the pseudobulbs. Generally, only a few pseudobulbs are formed: one, two or four, according to the species. Many terrestrial orchids such as those of the *Orchis* or *Ophrys* genera, whose leaves and stems disappear during the cold season, have other storage organs. These are two bulbs in amongst the roots: one is shrivelled, having provided the resources for the plant to develop; the other is newly formed, ready to nourish the new leaves and stems in spring. It is to these two tubers lying side by side, incidentally, that the orchid owes its name: the Greek word *orchis* means testicle.

In climates where warmth and humidity remain constant, and there is thus no need for storage organs, some terrestrial orchids manage without. They also have no stem, just leaves and floral spikes. The best known of these are the *Paphiopedilum* orchids.

Monopodial orchids

The stems of these orchids get longer and longer and may, like vanilla (a liana), reach several metres. Most, however, remain within reasonable limits, as in plants of the genera* *Vanda, Phalaenopsis, Angraecum, Aerides,* and others. The leaves are arranged alternately around the stem. Roots are found at the base, and here and there along the length of the stem.

Great diversity of leaf form

The orchid leaf is always simple, with longitudinal veins, but even so a wide diversity of forms is to be found between species. They may be oval or lanceolate, they may form thin strips, or be long and cylindrical, and so on; they may be vast or minute, or even completely absent.

Species that grow in the sun have thick leaves (*Cattleya, Oncidium splendidum, Dendrobium linguiforme,* etc.), whereas those from shady habitats have thin ones. Apart from a few exceptions (for example *Eria velutina*), orchid leaves are not hairy. They sometimes take on the same role as pseudobulbs, that of water storage organs, as in *Epidendrum parkinsonianum, Phalaenopsis gigantea,* or in the *Pleurothallis,* where pseudobulbs are lacking.

Although the leaves are usually some shade of green, other colours do occur. In *Phalaenopsis schilleriana,* for example, the lower leaf surface is violet, and in *Macodes petola* the leaves are veined with golden yellow.

Above

Neottia nidus-avis (Bird's Nest Orchid) (× 1.2)

Highly sophisticated roots

Although the roots of terrestrial orchids are unremarkable compared with those of other plants, quite the opposite is true of epiphyte root systems. All root systems serve to take in water and mineral salts but this is more difficult in the air than in the ground. The roots of tree orchids have therefore evolved and diversified far more. They are usually cylindrical in form, and may hang down several metres to capture moisture from the air. For this purpose, the external surface of the roots is covered in a spongy tissue called velamen, which gives them their silvery grey hue. An orchid perched high on a branch could only too easily be dislodged by an animal or a puff of wind, and fall from its tree, so the second function of these robust roots is to anchor the plant solidly onto its support. In leafless orchids (*Microcoelia, Chiloschista, Taeliophyllum*), they serve a third function, using the chlorophyll they contain to take over the task of photosynthesis from the absent leaves.

With all these morphological variations the orchid is clearly a highly versatile plant, able to adapt to many environments. Indeed, orchids are found almost everywhere.

The orchid has colonized the world

Orchids are found on every continent except Antarctica, and in every habitat other than desert. They are even found in regions of low temperature and high humidity, such as Uruguay (e.g. *Oncidium bifolium*). *Dendrobium cunninghamii*, which grows in New Zealand, is sometimes exposed to freezing conditions; the *Dendrobium* orchids of Tasmania and Australia grow on rocks and are hence known as lithophytes*. At latitudes close to our own, the Alps and Pyrenees possess a magnificent orchid flora, which are all terrestrial, while closer to the equator, epiphytes are most common. Orchids are plentiful at altitudes of 1,100 to 2,100 m (3,600 to 6,900 ft).

White flowers are most numerous in Africa, while in Asia, the continent which boasts the most species, the flowers are multicoloured. Orchids on the American continent are equally rich in colour; this is the favoured territory of the *Cattleya*. Papua has beautiful, uniquely coloured examples of *Dendrobium*. Southern China, with its Himalayan flora, possesses some remarkable examples of *Paphiopedilum*, and another interesting terrestrial flora grows in Australia.

It is a strange fact that certain genera grow in only one region of the world and nowhere else, even if identical conditions exist elsewhere. For example, the *Odontoglossum genus* is only found in South America; the Vanda genus colonizes only South East Asia, and so on.

With such beauty, such curious features and such a wide distribution, the orchid was destined to be exploited by man.

A plant with a multiplicity of uses

The use to which popular medicine put certain orchids may readily be imagined from the suggestive shape of their paired underground tubers. Today in Turkey, *salep* is still prepared from dried orchid roots. Vanilla, which was used by the Aztecs, is cultivated more than any other orchid in the world. Its wonderfully aromatic pods are used to flavour many foods, and in perfumes. It is an important source of national income in the main producing countries, such as Madagascar, the Comoros, and Reunion Island, though the market for natural vanillin is considerably smaller than that for the

artificial product. Let us hope that it will not be entirely supplanted.

In China, the pseudobulbs of certain species of *Dendrobium* are used in a sedative infusion. In Korea, *Dendrobium nobile* has been found to contain anti-cancer agents. Throughout Asia, the flower plays a key role in everyday life and in religious practices. For the Australian Aborigines the fruit of the *Cymbidium* is a contraceptive. In the Antilles, *Bletia tuberosa* is used to treat poisoning. In Japan, the sap of *Bletilla* produces a glue used in traditional crafts. In Guatemala and Peru, orchids feature in religious ceremonies as offerings and decorations. For Guatemalans, *Cattleya skinneri* is the flower of Saint Sebastian, while in Costa Rica it is the national flower. In Panama *Peristeria elata* takes this place of honour.

As in the past, orchids continue to inspire painters, sculptors and others, and for the rest of us they arouse admiration, at the very least.

Since 1698, when the first tropical orchid, *Brassavola nodosa*, was brought back to Holland from the island of Curaçao, the attraction of these flowers has grown steadily. At first, they were known only to those fortunate enthusiasts who could mount expeditions to bring back plant material for their collections. Gradually, however, as methods of cultivation improved, and in particular, cheaper methods of heating, based on steam rather than hot air, were introduced, tropical orchids became accessible to a wider public. Since the end of the nineteenth century, orchids have been cultivated on a large scale for the cut flower trade in the Ghent area of Belgium. Ghent exports *Cattleya*, *Odontoglossum* and *Paphiopedilum* to Paris and Berlin, and even Moscow. In England, the cradle of orchid collections, it would have been the norm for a stately home or any elegant middle-class dwelling to have at least one orchid house. Collections are still flourishing, and orchids are sold at auction

Above

Dendrobium speciosum (× 0.8)

Introduction

11

like works of art. In the United States, Germany, and France, we find the same infatuation. All the great horticulturists are taking up the cultivation of orchids.

The Netherlands are currently the premier European orchid producer. In the tropical regions of the world, Thailand was the first to develop their cultivation, but Malaysia has the largest area devoted to orchid production. Japan is the world's principal importer of cut flowers, while the largest in Europe is Italy. Orchid imports into France in 1993 totalled eight million stems. This flourishing trade is not limited to botanical species – quite the contrary. They are mainly hybrid species, created by horticulturists in their hundreds of thousands. These may simply be the result of crossing two related species, but can also be hybrids of two or even three to four different genera (*Vuylstekeara = Cochlioda × Miltonia × Odontoglossum. Burrageara = Cochlioda × Miltonia × Odontoglossum × Oncidium*).

Though for cultivated orchids the future seems secure, the situation is quite different for those species, known or unknown, which still persist in the wild. Their habitats are threatened by the large-scale destruction of tropical forests and, closer to home, by the breakneck speed of urbanization. Many orchids will not survive this, but let us hope that, in a few years, man will have become less destructive, and may still, in some remote corner of forest, chance upon a new species of this marvellous flower.

above
Ada aurantiaca (× 1.35)

Of the two species of this genus, only the one shown here is cultivated. It has been crossed to create two new genera, *Adaglossa* (*Ada* × *Odontoglossum*) and *Adioda* (*Ada* × *Cochlioda*). The plant comes from Columbia, where it grows at an altitude of 2,000 m (6,600 ft). It prefers the cool house and flowers mainly in winter.

Facing page
Aerangis biloba (× 0.85)

This genus takes its name from the Greek *aer* (air) and *angos* (urn), an allusion to the shape of the labellum. It grows widely in Africa, and comprises 60 species, which are easy to cultivate in an intermediate or hot house. This example is an epiphyte from West Africa and strongly resembles the Kenyan species *Aerangis fuscatum*. It bears abundant flowers, and is grown on a slab of cork bark. It requires a resting period between June and August.

Left
Aerangis germinyanum (×0.8)

This small, bushy plant originates from the Comoros and is cultivated in the hot house, grown either on a slab of cork bark or in a pot. The 4 cm (1 ½ in) flowers appear in winter or spring and occasionally even in autumn. It is propagated by division in spring.

Right
Angulocaste Olympus (×0.75)

This is a hybrid between *Anguloa* and *Lycaste* (*Angulocaste* Apollo × *Lycaste* Sunrise), created in 1950 by Wyldcourt in England. It is cultivated in the intermediate house.

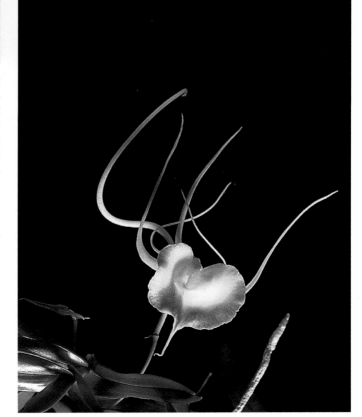

Left

Arpophyllum spicatum (× 0.6)

This is an epiphytic genus from Central America, described in 1825 by Llave and Lexarza. The name comes from the Greek *arpo* (sickle) and *phyllum* (leaf). Five species are known, with a distribution stretching from Mexico to Colombia. This species is Mexican. Cultivation is in intermediate or cool house conditions. In winter, it should be kept dry, without allowing it to dry out completely.

Ascocentrum miniatum (× 1.35)

This dwarf epiphyte from tropical Asia is much appreciated by amateurs. It is found in Thailand, Burma, Malaysia and the Philippines. The name comes from the Greek *askos* (wine skin) and *kentron* (spur), an allusion to its swollen spur. It has given rise to a number of hybrids through crossing with *Vanda*, *Aerides*, *Trichoglottis*, *Ascoglossum*, *Renanthera*, and others, to produce new genera such as *Lewisara*, *Robinara*, *Christieara*, *Kagawara*, *Mokara*, *Vascostylis*, etc. They all require a good deal of light, and are easy to cultivate indoors or in a hot house.

Bepi orchidglades (× 1.55)

This is a cross between *Brassavola nodosa* and *Epidendrum schomburgkii*, which grows vigorously in a hot to intermediate house. It produces many offshoots, which are repotted when their roots reach a length of 3 cm (1 $^1/_4$ in). Care should be taken to keep it slightly damp, but not dry. It flowers almost the whole year.

above.

Bletia purpurea (× 1.5)

This genus is named in honour of Luis Blet, the Spanish botanist. The plants, including both epiphytes and terrestrial species, come from tropical America. This example is grown in an intermediate house, and requires a short resting period between August and September. Its main enemy is the red spider mite. A mixture of peat or sand with rotted oak or beech leaves is used for repotting. Spring-flowering.

Brassia ochoroleuca (× 0.4)

A genus of 20 species growing in tropical America, from Florida to Argentina. It is named after William Brass, the artist who drew the plants collected by Sir Joseph Banks. The species is easy to cultivate in an intermediate house, in a mixture of peat and pine bark or on a slab of cork bark. It is important to give it just enough water in winter to prevent it from drying out. Winter-flowering.

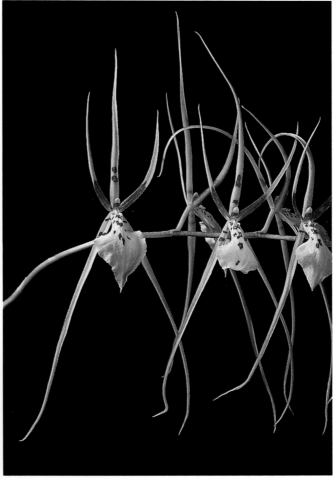

Brassavola flagellaris (× 0.95)

Created by the English botanist R. Brown, this genus was named in honour of a Venetian gentleman, Antonio Musa Brassavola, and comprises fifteen species. This one is native to Brazil, and is easy to cultivate in an intermediate house. It can be grown on a slab of cork bark, or in a suspended earthenware pot. It flowers in autumn.

Left
Brassocattleya Déesse
'Perfection' (×0.7)

This is a bigeneric* hybrid between *Brassocattleya* Ferrières and *Cattleya* Lamartine, created by Vacherot in 1947. *Brassocattleya* Ferrières is a cross between *Brassavola digbyana* and *Cattleya* Dionysius, created by Chassaing, head gardener of the Château de Ferrières in the French region of Brie. *Cattleya* Dionysius is a cross in which the species *Cattleya warscewiczii* is dominant. It flowers from the end of September to October, in an intermediate to hot house. Grown indoors, it requires plenty of light and watering once a week.

Facing page
Bulbophyllum bequaertii (×2.25)

The name of this genus, created in 1822 by M. Aubert du Petit Thouars, is derived from the Greek *bolbos* (bulb) and *phyllum* (leaf). It is found in all the tropical regions of the world, especially in Asia and Oceania. Today it comprises 1,200 species, divided into several groups, the best-known being *Cirrhopetalum*. They are epiphytic plants with pseudobulbs and a single leaf. This African species is found in Zaire and in the Kakamega forest in Kenya. Grown on a slab of cork bark in a hot to intermediate house, it flowers almost the entire year.

above

Bulbophyllum umbellatum

(× 1)

A variable species native to several regions. This example comes from the Philippines. It should be grown in a pot, half shaded in summer and well watered, and flowers between April and June in an intermediate house.

Left
Bulbophyllum ornatissimum
(× 1.2)

Better known under the name *Cirrho-petalum ornatissimum*, this plant comes from Assam in India. It is grown on cork bark or in a pot in the intermediate house, where it flowers in the autumn. It should be kept moist all year round.

Bulbophyllum Louis Sander

(× 1) (× 0.75)

(× 0.55) (× 0.35)

(× 1)

A hybrid created in 1936 by the legendary family of orchid-fanciers, then established at St Albans in England and Bruges in Belgium, by crossing *Bulbophyllum longissimum* and *Bulbophyllum ornatissimum.* It is easy to cultivate in an intermediate to hot house, and flowers in autumn. It should be kept moist all year round.

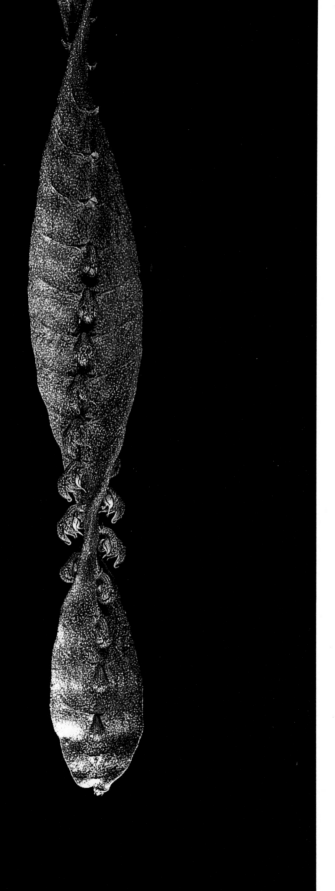

Right
Bulbophyllum fuscopurpureum

(× 1)

This is a vigorous plant from Rwanda, which grows in damp forest in the Parc National des Volcans. It needs to be cultivated in a hot house and kept moist all year round. Flowering occurs in spring.

Calanthe elmeri (× 1)

From the Greek *kalis* (beautiful) and *anthos* (flower), this genus of 150 species is unevenly distributed across the globe, from South Africa and Madagascar to Australia and Tahiti, by way of the Indies, Japan, Indonesia, and New Caledonia. The plants are terrestrial, and divided into two groups: those which lose their leaves and those which retain them. This species originates from the Philippines, where it is found from sea level up to an altitude of 1,800 m (5,900 ft). It flowers between January and April. It needs to be repotted every year, well watered, and given plenty of fertilizer as it grows; all feeding is stopped from August and it must be kept slightly moist in winter. It can be grown in a hot house, or indoors.

Right
Calanthe rosea (× 1.15)

This terrestrial plant from Thailand is one which loses its leaves. Grown in hot house conditions, it requires good feeding and plenty of light during its growing period. During flowering, water should be reduced; after flowering, it should be stopped altogether. The plant needs to be kept dry until the end of March.

Left

Cattleya guatemalensis (× 0.7)

A natural hybrid between *Cattleya auran-tiaca* and *Cattleya skinneri*, this orchid is the national flower of Guatemala. Colour varies considerably, from garnet through to deep yellow. It should be grown in an intermediate house, avoiding excessive watering in winter. Spring-flowering.

Right

Cattleya bicolor (× 0.7)

Voluptuous and exotic, the genus *Cattleya* embodies the glory of the orchid more than any other. It was described in 1821 by Lindley, and named in honour of William Cattley, the famous orchid-fancier. Examples, found throughout tropical America, are divided into two groups: the bifoliates and the unifoliates. The former are Mexican and Brazilian; the latter come from Panama, Colombia, Peru, Venezuela and Brazil. These orchids owed their popularity in the early years of the twentieth century mainly to the beauty of their flowers. This species comes from Brazil; it has been used for many years to produce new hybrids. It is cultivated in an intermediate house, with 50 per cent light in summer and full light in winter. Care should be taken to avoid over-watering in winter.

Facing page

Cattleya guttata (× 2.2)

A plant of great beauty, reaching a height of 70 to 100 cm (27 to 39 in). Several varieties exist, of which the most famous is *Cattleya guttata v. leopoldii*. This species was introduced into Europe in 1827 by Robert Gordon. It should be grown in intermediate to hot house conditions, and it flowers in summer.

Right

Coelogyne cristata (× 0.6)

Certainly the most cultivated of all *Coelogyne* species, this orchid originates from the Himalayas, where it grows on northwest-facing rocks in full sun or in very open forest, at an altitude of 1,600 to 2,700 metres (5,200 to 8,900 feet). Winters there are often cool and fairly dry. From June onwards, the monsoon brings several months of heavy rain. The plant consequently needs plenty of water and feeding in summer, and almost full sun. A low temperature and slightly moist growing medium are recommended in winter. It flowers between February and March.

Above

Cattleya labiata v. *warneri* (× 0.9)

Synonym: *Cattleya warneri*. The *labiata* species has many varieties, and is regarded as a group in itself by certain specialists. Thousands of hybrids have been created from it, and it is still a very popular plant, often used by orchid-lovers. It is grown in pine bark or in a pot, in an intermediate house, and flowers in autumn. Allow time between waterings in winter.

Coelogyne fimbriata (× 1.2)

From the Greek *koilos* (hollow) and *gune* (organ), the *Coelogyne* genus was established by Lindley, and comprises 200 species, distributed from the Indies to the Pacific Ocean. This one comes from Thailand. It is a small but very vigorous plant, cultivated in an intermediate house or indoors, in a pot or on a slab of cork bark. It should be kept moist all year round. Autumn-flowering.

The genus *Cymbidium* was established by Olof Swartz in 1799. It comprises 50 species, distributed across tropical Asia, in India, China, Japan, and Australia. The name comes from *kumbos* (cavity), referring to the shape of the labellum. The genus possesses some beautiful, large-flowered species, which have been and still are being used in horticulture to produce numerous hybrids. This species, from the north of Thailand, is an epiphyte with pendant flowers. It should be cultivated in hanging pots in a hot house, where it flowers in summer.

Right
Dactylorhiza maculata (× 0.65)

The name of this Eurasian genus comes from the Greek *dactulos* (finger) and *rhiza* (root). Its 49 species are distributed across an area from Scandinavia to North Africa, taking in the Himalayas, Madeira, Iceland, and even Alaska. This species grows in the marshes, moorlands, and lightly wooded areas of our own regions. It is a protected plant, so we must be content just to admire it.

Facing page
Coelogyne speciosa (× 2)

This hot house plant originates from Indonesia. Its curious, large flowers emerge as autumn turns to winter, but with skill it can be made to flower in June. Watering can be reduced once the pseudobulb is mature.

Above and right

Dendrobium amabile (× 0.55 and × 0.4)

Synonym: *Dendrobium bronckartii.* Established in 1799 by the Swede Olof Swartz, the *Dendrobium* genus takes its name from the Greek *dendron* (tree) and *bios* (life), i.e. tree-living. Today more than 200-300 species are distributed over an area stretching from the temperate regions of Japan to Australia, the tropical regions of Asia and also New Zealand (*Dendrobium cunninghamii*), where winter nights are very cold. This species, which comes from Vietnam, should be cultivated in an intermediate house. If winter temperatures are too low, it should be kept dry. It flowers in spring.

Dendrobium anosmum (× 1)

This species is found in Malaysia, Vietnam, and the Philippines (in the Banaue region of the province of Luzon, near the famous ricefields). A different type of *Dendrobium anosmum* is found along the mountainous Thai–Malay border. Cultivation of this epiphyte is carried out in an intermediate house, on a slab of cork bark or in a hanging basket. It should be kept slightly damp in winter and dry from March, until the first fortnight in April. Spring-flowering.

Right

Dendrobium arachnites (× 2)

Small, epiphytic plant from Thailand and Burma. It should be cultivated in a hot house, or even an intermediate house, grown on a slab of cork bark, and kept less moist from February to March.

This species differs from others of the *Dendrobium* genus. It is widely distributed in the east of Java, at an altitude of 1,200 to 1,800 metres (3,900 to 5,900 feet), and is also found in India, Burma, and Malaysia, growing on the branches of isolated trees. It is cultivated in an intermediate house, and should be kept slightly moist in winter. Flowers in autumn.

This species is the most popular of the entire genus. It originates from the mountainous regions of India, as well as the Himalayan chain. Alternating between the cool house and the intermediate house, cultivation is simple: plenty of light, watering, and feeding, after flowering. From July to March, no nitrogenous fertilizer should be given. The plants should be put in the cool house in October; in January, they are transferred back to the intermediate house, where the flower buds open four or five weeks later. Water in moderation.

The first hybrids were obtained by English orchid-growers; over the last thirty years, the most beautiful ones have come from Japan.

This very vigorous Australian plant bears its flowers in long spikes. It is cultivated in a cool house, and kept slightly moist. The temperature from November onwards should be kept as low as cool house conditions permit, around 10°C (50°F). These conditions induce proper flowering at the end of winter.

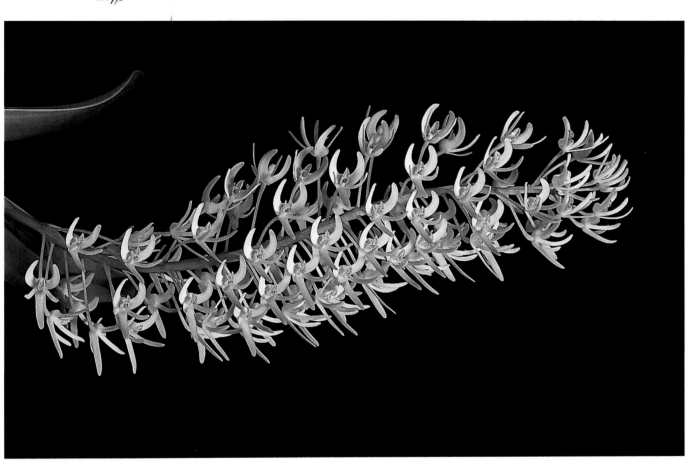

above
Dendrobium speciosum (× 0.5)

Dendrochilum glumaceum (× 1.15)

From the Greek *dendro* (tree) and *chilos* (lip), this genus consists of 150 species distributed across South East Asia. This one comes from the Philippines, where it grows on rocks and trees. It is cultivated in an intermediate house.

Left

Dendrobium tenuissimum

This epiphytic species from the coasts of New South Wales and the humid forests of Queensland in Australia, where it grows at an altitude of 1,000 m (3,300 ft). It should be grown on a slab of cork bark in intermediate to cool house conditions, and flowers in spring.

Synonym: 'Pride of Table Mountain'. The most beautiful of the terrestrial orchids of South Africa, its Latin name alludes to the flower's rich coloration. The genus has 133 species. It grows in gorges, along waterfalls and streams, in shade or full sun, at an altitude of 1,000 to 1,200 metres (3,300 to 3,900 feet). *Disa* orchids are difficult to cultivate, though a few orchid-fanciers do obtain good results. The mineralogical composition of the growing medium is the main source of difficulty.

Right

Doritis pulcherrima (× 0.75)

From the Greek *dory* (lance), an allusion to the pointed labellum, or from Doritis, the other name for Aphrodite. This genus has only one species, but many varieties. It is an Asian epiphyte, found from India to the Philippines. Cultivation is in intermediate to hot house conditions. It is much used for hybridization, being crossed with *Phalaenopsis* to produce the bigeneric hybrid *Doritaenopsis*. Flowering is from August to November.

Facing page

Dendrochilum magnum (× 0.65)

This epiphyte from the Luzon province of the Philippines is a strong plant with long leaves, and an inflorescence of great beauty. It is cultivated in an intermediate house in semi-shade.

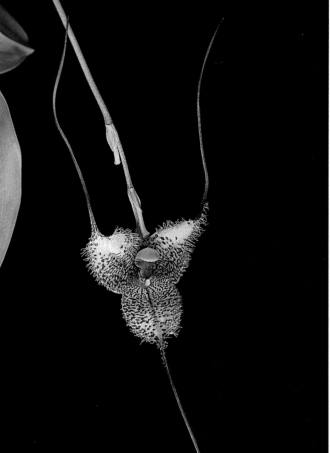

Right
Encyclia brassavolae (× 1)

This genus from tropical America consists of 150 species. Its name comes from the Greek *enkyklein* (to encircle), a reference to the labellum, which encircles the column. It generally thrives in sunny areas, in open forest, in Mexico and Guatemala, and is best cultivated in a cool house, with plenty of air and light. As with the entire *Encyclia* genus, it should be kept dry in winter. Summer-flowering.

Left
Dracula chimaera (× 0.75)

Genus established by Carlyle A. Luer in 1978, the date at which it was distinguished from *Masdevallia*. Its sixty species are native to the Andes, and should be cultivated in a cool house. It needs either good shading during the summer months, or creation of an artificial mist in daytime. This species is a very attractive little plant, with remarkably beautiful flowers. It flowers in summer and winter.

This epiphyte grows in Mexico, the Caribbean, and as far south as Venezuela. It is quite common in cultivation, being easy to grow; it flowers from March to November in an intermediate house, or even indoors.

Preceding double page and right

Epidendrum ibaguense

(× 1.7; × 1.7; × 1.7)

(× 1.7; × 1.7; × 1.7)

(× 0.9)

Synonym: *Epidendrum radicans*. This plant of 30 sub-species grows in Panama, along Bolivian roadways, and in the Chanchamayo valley in Peru. It shows great variation in different sites and geographical areas. It is cultivated in all tropical countries, and used as a cut flower and for decoration. Grown in an intermediate house or indoors, it needs plenty of light (almost full sun). Flowering is from March to November. The most widespread hybrid is *Epidendrum obrienianum* (*Epidendrum radicans × Epidendrum erectum*, 1888).

Epidendrum pseudepidendrum

(× 1)

All the *Epidendrum* species are American. There is a great variety of forms, both terrestrial and epiphytic, and altogether 500 species. The name comes from the Greek *epi* (on) and *dendron* (tree). This species can reach a height of 2.5 m (8 ft). It is cultivated in a hot house with plenty of light, and flowers from March to October.

Below

Epipactis atrorubens (× 3.15)

This genus of 36 species is Eurasian, but includes one American and one African species. Examples are found in the temperate regions of Europe. This species is fairly common, and grows in wide open clearings, or in undergrowth on calcareous soils (semi-shade to full sun). This plant is not one to be grown in gardens, but to be admired in its natural setting; it is protected.

Right

Dendrolirium altidolomentosum

(× 0.55)

Formerly named *Eria*, an alternative name *Dendrolirium* was proposed by Carl Blume in 1825 and accepted as being more appropriate. It consists of 13 species from East Asia, Malaysia, Indonesia, and Vietnam. This hot-house epiphyte flowers in autumn.

Laelia crispata (× 0.6)

This genus, named in honour of Caius Laelius, is very similar to *Cattleya*, but has a different number of pollinia: the *Cattleya* genus has four, *Laelia* eight. *Laelia* and *Cattleya* are often crossed to produce the genus *Laeliocattleya*. This species is an epiphyte from Brazil. It should be cultivated in an intermediate house, where it normally flowers in autumn, and occasionally also in spring.

Laelia pumila (× 0.85)

This Brazilian species is found in the region of the Paraiba river delta, in the northern part of the state of Rio de Janeiro and in the states of Espirito Santo and Minas Gerais. It grows high up in the tree tops, as well as along small waterfalls, where the sky is often misted over. It is best cultivated in an intermediate house with plenty of light, and kept slightly moist in winter. Autumn-flowering.

Right

Ticoglossum bictonense (×1.34)

In 1984, the Mexican botanist Halbinger was able to distinguish this genus from *Odontoglossum*. This species is native to Mexico, Guatemala and Salvador. It is an intermediate-house epiphyte, needing semi-shade. It has been used to create some forty hybrids with *Brassia*, *Oncidium*, *Miltonia*, etc. In Mediterranean regions, it can be cultivated outside, in the shade, from April to November. It flowers in autumn.

Facing page

Leptotes bicolor (×3.9)

This small Brazilian genus, from the state of Minas Gerais, consists of only two species. The tiny plant produces beautiful flowers in autumn–winter, and is best cultivated on a slab of cork bark or in a small pot, in pine bark, in an intermediate house. Avoid over-watering in winter.

Right
Lockhartia oerstedii (× 1)

This genus was named in honour of David Lockhart, superintendent of the Royal Botanic Garden in Trinidad. An American genus comprising thirty species, it has a tropical and sub-tropical distribution stretching from Mexico to Bolivia. This epiphyte of dense and humid forests grows at an altitude of 1,100 m (3,600 ft). It is cultivated on a slab of cork bark or in a small pot, in an intermediate house. Generous watering and damping down are needed in summer. It flowers from spring to autumn.

Left
Listrostachys pertusa (× 0.55)

From the Greek listron (plough) and sta-chus (spike). This is an epiphyte from the humid forests of tropical Africa (Sierra Leone, Togo, and Zaire) where it grows in the semi-shade of trees. It should be cultivated in a pot, in hot house conditions, and flowers in winter.

Synonym: *Haemeria discolor*. This is a small, terrestrial orchid from Asia. It is a very decorative plant, easy to cultivate in a hot house and to propagate by cuttings (in September). It should be grown in a small pot or in a basket, in a mixture of moss and sand, or of sphagnum peat and leaf mould from beech or oak leaves. Most importantly, it should be kept well shaded. It is a favourite for cultivation and propagation in the Netherlands, and is winter-flowering.

This epiphyte is native to Central America, growing at an altitude of 2,000 m (6,600 ft) in Honduras, Guatemala, El Salvador, and the Chiapas mountains. It has given rise to beautiful hybrids with many colour variations. It should be culti-vated in an intermediate house, avoiding excessive wetness in winter. Flowering is from December to June.

above
Lycaste skinneri (× 1.2)

Facing page
Masdevallia coccinea (× 2.43)

Named in honour of José Masdevall, the eighteenth-century Spanish botanist, this genus consists of 275 species, which flourish at an altitude of 2,500 to 4,000 m (8,200 to 13,100 ft) in the Cordilleras of the Andes. This species grows in Colombia and Venezuela, at 3,000 m (9,800 ft). It is popular with orchid-lovers and often grown for cut flowers. It should be culti-vated in a cool house, and kept moist. Its flowering season is from summer to winter.

Right

Masdevallia infracta (×2.5)

This small plant from Brazil exists in a number of variations. It is easy to culti-vate in an intermediate house, where it should be kept moist all year round. It flowers from autumn to winter.

Facing page

Masdevallia ignea (×2.35)

This lovely, hardy species from Colombia has given rise to some beautiful hybrids. It is cultivated in a cool house, avoiding excessive summer heat. It should be well shaded. Winter-flowering.

Right ***Masdevallia kimballiana*** (×2)

This hybrid of *Masdevallia caudata* and *Masdevallia veitchiana* was created in 1893 by Sander of St Albans in England. It grows easily, produces plenty of leaves and flowers, and is much appreciated by orchid-lovers. Grown in a cool house, it flowers almost all year round.

Masdevallia polysticta (× 1.3)

This Peruvian plant grows at an altitude of 2,500 m (8,200 ft). It is remarkable for its flower spikes* (many flowers on each stem). It should be cultivated in a pot, in cool conditions, and repotted frequently, as it grows taller and taller. It flowers in winter and in spring.

Facing page
Miltonioides warscewiczii (×3)

Synonym: *Oncidium warscewiczii*. Having been classified under various genera in the past, this species has now been placed in a genus all of its own. It is an epiphyte from Costa Rica, and is crossed with *Oncidium*, *Brassia*, *Odontoglossum* and *Aspasia*. It is grown in an intermediate house, half-shaded, where it flowers in summer and autumn.

Right
Maxillaria elegantula (×0.85)

From the Latin *maxilla* (jaw), a reference to the shape of the labellum. It is very difficult to describe the genus *Maxillaria*, since it encompasses more than 250 species. Peru alone has 32, Colombia 65, and French Guiana 30. Distribution stretches from Florida, through all the tropical and sub-tropical countries, down to Argentina. This cool house species should be kept slightly moist in winter. It flowers in autumn.

Left
Masdevallia veitchiana (×0.7)

This plant is the most beautiful of all the *Masdevallia* genus. It grows at an altitude of 3,500 m (11,500 ft) in the Urubamba and Machu Picchu regions of Peru. It needs ample humidity and shade in summer to avoid excessive heat. It has given rise to some beautiful hybrids.

Right

Neobenthamia gracilis (× 1.35)

This terrestrial orchid, native to Tanzania, can reach a height of 2 m (6 ½ ft). It forms a cluster of terminal flowers, and thrives in full sun. It should be grown in intermediate to cool conditions, and flowers in autumn and winter, after a short resting period.

A strong, terrestrial plant with large pseudobulbs and leaves a metre (3 ft) long, named in honour of F. Moore, curator of the Botanic Garden at Glasnevin, Dublin. It comes from the mountainous regions of Panama and Colombia, and is grown in a hot house. Given a resting period from October to December, it will flower from February to April.

Right

Odontoglossum pulchellum (× 1.2)

From the Greek *odonto* (tooth) and *glossa* (tongue), referring to the shape of the labellum. This American genus, comprising 58 species, has a wide distribution stretching from Mexico to Bolivia. A large number of the Mexican species has been transferred to the genus *Lemboglossum*, and this plant is included under *Osmoglossum* by some botanists. It is a small, Central American plant which grows in open, but cool and humid, forest, with a dry period. It is best cultivated in a cool house, in not too big a pot, and should be well watered during growth but less in winter. Flowering is from March to May.

Below

Osvaldella centradenia (× 1.6)

Named in honour of the Danish botanist
A.S. Oersted, this small genus from
Central America comprises eighteen
species. The nomenclature varies from
author to author. The species shown is
an epiphyte with large roots in propor-
tion to its size. It prefers half-shade in
an intermediate house, and should not
be over-watered in winter. It flowers in
winter and spring.

Left

Odontoglossum humilum (× 0.25)

This is one of the many Peruvian species
which flourish at high altitude, in cloud
forest. The flower spikes are long, with
curious small flowers. It should be grown
in a cool house, keeping it slightly moist
all year round. Autumn-flowering.

Oncidium blanchettii (× 1.75)

This genus was established by Olof Swartz in 1793, based on his description of *Oncidium altissimum*. The name, from the Greek *onkos* (tumour), refers to the warts on the labellum. Since then, the number of species belonging to the *Oncidium* genus has been the subject of continual debate on the part of prominent botanists, and remains an open question. It is an American genus, distributed across all the tropical and sub-tropical regions of the continent, and displays enormous diversity: some grow high in the trees of the Amazon, and others in southern Brazil where winters can be harsh. They may be terrestrial or epiphytic. This Brazilian species nestles in the rocks of the mountains of Minas Gerais. It is grown in a cool house, needs slight watering in winter, and flowers in autumn.

Oncidium carthagenense (× 2)

This is a widely distributed species with small pseudobulbs and large leaves, which grows in open forest between 500 and 1,000 m (1,650 and 3,300 ft). It displays considerable variation, according to its geographical position. It should be grown in a hanging basket or on a slab of cork bark, in an intermediate to hot house. The flowers appear on long stems in summer.

A beautiful species from Peru and Colombia, which grows easily in the greenhouse. It flowers in autumn, producing a long flower spike, dotted with clusters of three to four flowers. It should be grown in a cool house, and watered with special care in winter.

Oncidium ornithorhynchum

(× 2)

This small plant from Central America forms beautiful clumps and produces flower spikes with copious, richly vanilla-scented flowers. It can be grown in an intermediate house, or even indoors. It has given rise to several hybrids, such as *Oncidium* Jamie Sutton. This was crossed with *Oncidium* Honolulu in 1983 to produce the hybrid *Oncidium* Sharry Baby.

Above

Ophrys bombyliflora (× 7)

The most handsome of the terrestrial orchids, the 50 species of this genus are found along the coasts of Europe from the South of Scandinavia to the North of Morocco, and from the Mediterranean Basin to the Caspian Sea. European regulations for nature conservation prohibit the trading or destruction of this plant. Spring-flowering.

above.

Ornithidium coccineum (× 2.15)

From the Greek *ornithidion* (little bird), this genus consists of 35 species. This one grows in the tropical mountains of Jamaica, Cuba, Trinidad, Peru, Colombia, and Brazil. Grown in a hot house, half-shaded, it needs a resting period to promote the formation of its flower buds, which open in winter.

Facing page

Paphiopedilum callosum (× 1.65)

The name of this genus is derived from the Greek Paphos, another name for Aphrodite or Venus, and *pedilon* (slipper). It was established by Pfitzer in 1903. Horticulturists have divided the genus into two groups: those with green leaves, which are intermediate to cool house plants, and those with mottled leaves, which need hot to intermediate conditions. This species, which is often cultivated, is native to Cambodia and central Thailand, and is a highly representative of the genus. It is a robust plant, and flowers well. It needs to be kept moist all year, with a minimum temperature of 12°C (54°F) by night, and 18°C (64°F) by day. Flowering is normally from February to March, but can be from August to October.

Left

Paphiopedilum esquirolei (× 0.8)

Introduced by Esquirol in 1912, this is seen by some authors as a variety of the species *hirsutissimum*. It is found in northern Thailand, and also in the Guizhou region of China. It is a hot-house plant, needing plenty of light and a resting period in winter. It should be kept slightly moist for six weeks in the winter. Flowering occurs between April and May. The *Paphiopedilum* genus groups together some sixty Asian species, which grow from the Himalayas to New Guinea and the Solomon Islands.

Right

Paphiopedilum henryanum (× 1)

This species was discovered some years ago in Southern China. Since then, many others have been found on the Guizhou plateau. This one comes from the heights of Na Po (a calcareous region) where summer temperatures reach 35°C (95°F). In winter, the temperature falls to 15°C (59°F), and may even become low enough for frost. The summers are rather dry, but there are heavy rains in autumn. This plant needs to be grown in an intermediate house, and flowers in November.

Paphiopedilum haynaldianum

(× 0.9)

This multiflorous species (many flowers on one stem) is native to the mountainous regions of the Philippine provinces of Luzon and Negros. It grows from sea level up to an altitude of 1,800 m (5,900 ft) on granite rocks and in the hills on calcareous soil, where it is exposed to a most extreme climate. This is cool and very humid in winter, with a great deal of sun from May to June, and copious rainfall from March to April; there follows less rain until the heavy monsoon at the end of August, and then frequent typhoons from September to October. Consequently, this plant needs high temperatures except in winter, and 50 per cent sunlight in summer.

above
Paphiopedilum malipoense
(× 0.65)

This is a beautiful, highly sought-after, intermediate-house species. Like *Paphiopedilum henryanum*, it comes from China, and requires the same conditions for its cultivation, but less watering in winter. It flowers in autumn.

Right
Paphiopedilum Onyx (× 1.3)

This hybrid was created by the firm of Vacherot, at Boissy-Saint-Léger, France, in 1945, by crossing *Paphiopedilum goultianum* and *Paphiopedilum* Maudiae. It is very vigorous, with beautiful mottled foliage, and is much used in the production of cut flowers. It flowers from autumn to winter.

Paphiopedilum rothschildianum
× *Paphiopedilum glaucophyllum*

(× 1)

This multiflorous hybrid is cultivated in a hot to intermediate house, where it grows slowly. It is not always easy to get it to flower, since the plant needs to be pushed to its maximum to flower well. The *rothschildianum* species is a native of Mount Kinabalu in Sabah, where it grows in full sun. The *glaucophyllum* species comes from Sumatra and Indonesia, adorning deep gorges with dense vegetation.

Peristeria elata (× 1)

This genus, native to tropical America, consists of seven species of which the national flower of Panama ('flower of the Holy Spirit') is the best known. The only terrestrial member of the genus, its flower spikes can reach a length of over a metre (3 feet), and bear very fragrant flowers. It should be grown in a hot house, taking care not to water the inside of the young shoots. It flowers between July and August.

Facing page

Paphiopedilum spicerianum

(× 2.45)

This species was introduced by the orchid-grower Hennis, of Hildesheim, Germany, in 1878. He found it in a consignment of *Paphiopedilum insigne*, imported from the Indies; both flower at the same time. It has been (and continues to be) much used for hybridization. It is best grown in an intermediate house, avoiding excessive watering in winter, when it flowers.

Above

Phalaenopsis amabilis (× 0.7)

This genus was described two centuries ago by C. Blume in Indonesia, and named from the Greek *phalaina* (moth) and *opsis* (resemble). It is found across the whole of South East Asia and even in Northern Australia. The example shown is cultivated more than any other orchid: millions of plants are produced all over the world, and much appreciated by the public for their long-lasting flowers. It is an ideal plant to grow indoors. The genus includes 50 species; the hybrids produced are all the result of selected crosses with *Phalaenopsis schilleriana* and *Phalaenopsis stuartiana*. It bears flowers all year, but most abundantly from February to April.

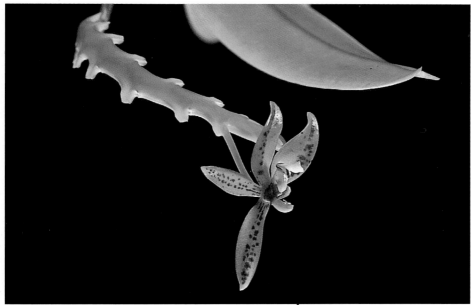

Right
Phalaenopsis cornu-cervi (× 1)

A native of Malaysia, Thailand, and Indonesia, this flower varies greatly depending on its geographical origin. It should be placed in the hot house, and the flower stem should not be cut, since it produces a succession of flowers over a period of months.

Left
Phalaenopsis amboinensis
(× 1)

This species, native to Indonesia, from Sulawesi (Celebes) and the island of Ambon, was seldom used for hybridization until about twenty years ago when many orchid growers hit upon it in their quest for a hybrid with pure yellow flowers. It blooms in summer and autumn.

Above

Phalaenopsis lueddemanniana

(× 1.25)

This Philippine epiphyte is found in almost every province of the archipelago. The species has many variations, regarded by some authors as species in their own right. It flowers all year in a hot house.

Right
Doritaenopsis Luminescent (× 0.85)

This hybrid between *Doritaenopsis* Rosina Pitta and *Phalaenopsis* William Sanders was produced in 1990 by Orchid Zone in the United States. The speckled variety of *Phalaenopsis* was first created in France but has been cultivated worldwide for some years now.

Above

Phalaenopsis leucorrhoda (× 0.7)

This species is a natural hybrid between
Phalaenopsis schilleriana and *Phalaenopsis
amabilis* v. *aphrodite*. It grows at low altitude in the provinces of Laguna,
Quezon and Rizal. Grown in the hot
house, it boasts not only beautiful
flowers, but also lovely foliage. Flowering
is in March–April.

Facing page

Phalaenopsis Oberhausen Gold

(× 1.6)

A cross between Golden Amboin and Golden Sands from 1988, this is one of numerous hybrids created to obtain new colours. The flowers are very beautiful, but not many are borne on each stem. It is a hot-house plant, and flowers there almost all year.

Above

Phalaenopsis speciosa
v. *tetraspis* (× 1.20)

The species was described by Reichenbach in 1874. For a long time, it was known only from illustrations and a herbal. Around a decade ago, the Indonesian collector Kolopaking redis-covered it on the northwestern tip of Sumatra (Aceh). It is easy to cultivate in a hot house, has attractive, shiny foliage, and flowers in autumn.

Right
Phragmipedium besseae (× 1.65)

The genus takes its name from the Greek *phragma* (partition) and *pedis* (foot). This species was discovered in 1981 by Libby Besse, following the allocation of concessions for petroleum research in the Napo region of Ecuador. It has been subject to trafficking and destruction through various abuses in its native habitat. It flowers in winter and spring.

This Asian genus consists of 40 species, spreading as far as New Caledonia and Australia. The species shown here is a robust plant, easy to cultivate in a hot or intermediate house, and flowering in autumn.

Right

Pleurothallis circumplexa (× 1.5)

This large tropical American genus is difficult to define, since according to some authors it is merely made up of 15 subgenera within the subtribe Pleurothallidinae. Nevertheless, there are 280 species, from 5 to 50 cm (2 to 20 in) in height: epiphytes, lithophytes and terrestrial. This species is grown in an intermediate house with good humidity. In winter, it should be kept slightly moist, but never dry. It flowers from February to October.

The cross between *Renanthera* and *Phalaenopsis* produces the genus *Renanthopsis*. This species is the product of *Renanthera monachica* and *Phalaenopsis stuartiana*, raised by Caroline Fort in Florida, in 1969. It should be grown in pine bark, in a hot house, where it flowers at least once during spring.

above

Renanthopsis Mildred Jameson

(× 0.9)

Below

Restrepia elegans (× 2.6)

Below

Restrepia elegans (× 2.6)

This genus is named in honour of Jose E. Restrepo, the Colombian naturalist, and comprises 28 species. The small, epiphytic plant depicted is found in tropical America, mainly in the Cordillera of the Andes. For cultivation, it should be placed in a cool house, half- to well-shaded, and kept moist in summer-autumn and slightly moist in winter. It flowers from spring until autumn.

Below

Sarcochilus hartmannii (× 1.6)

The genus was established by R. Brown in 1810, and named from the Greek *sarcos* (fleshy) and *cheilos* (lip), on account of its labellum. Whether it is Asian, or only Australian, still remains to be resolved. The majority of species come from eastern Australia. There are epiphytes and lithophytes, but also some almost saprophytic* terrestrial species with enormous roots. This plant is strong and vigorous, and is grown in a pot, in an intermediate house after flowering, until October, and in a cool house in winter. It should be well watered from spring to autumn, and will then flower freely from March to May.

Sauroglossum nitidum (× 1.35)

Synonym: *Spiranthes acaulis*. The plant photographed was brought back from the Urubamba valley, where it was found growing among plantings of coca. The flower spike reaches a length of 80 cm (30 in). It is a terrestrial plant, very common in the Andes, and easy to grow in a cool or intermediate house. It is found under various names: *Sauroglossum elatum, Sarcoglottis, Cyclopogon,* and *Satyrium.*

Above

Seidenfadenia mitrata (× 1.3)

The genus was established in 1872 by the American Garay, and named in honour of the Danish diplomat and botanist, Gunnar Seidenfaden. There is only one species which is found in Burma and Thailand, and it was known for a long time as *Aerides mitrata*. It is grown on a slab of cork bark, in a hot house, where it flowers in summer.

Sobralia fimbriata (× 1.3)

The *Sobralia* genus, from tropical America, comprises terrestrial to epiphytic plants, resembling bamboos, with a terminal inflorescence. The flowers last only two days, but appear in succession. This species is native to the Andean chain, in the Huánuco region of Peru. It is an epiphyte, little found in cultivation. In an intermediate house, it flowers in summer.

Right

Sophrolaeliocattleya

Hazel Boyd (×1.3)

A trigeneric hybrid created by Rod McLellan Co in 1975, this is the result of a cross between *Sophrolaeliocattleya* California Apricot with *Sophrolae-liocattleya* Jewel Box. The first of the parents had also been produced by McLellan in 1964, while the second was a 1962 product of Stewart Inc. These two Californian firms are very famous for their beautiful hybrids. Flowering is in spring, though some clones flower in autumn.

Spathoglottis plicata (× 1.15 and × 3)

This genus is dispersed throughout South East Asia, the islands of the Pacific, and Australia. It takes its name from the Greek *spatha* (spathe) and *glotta* (tongue), referring to the shape of the labellum. Its 49 species are found from sea level to an altitude of 3,000 m (9,800 ft). They are terrestrial plants, and should be grown in the greenhouse, slightly shaded, with plenty of moisture all year. This is the best known and most widespread species, and has many variations. In overcast weather, in the greenhouse, the flower pollinates itself, producing great numbers of young plants in neighbouring pots.

Right

Pleinanthes sinensis (× 2.6)

This species, as its name indicates, comes from China. The usual place to find it, however, is in the sphagnum moss used to repot *Paphiopedilums*. Some authors view it as a pink variation of *Spiranthes aestivalis*. It flowers in spring in a cool house.

L.C. Richard established this genus in 1818. Its name, from the Greek *speiros* (spiral) and *anthos* (flower), refers to the flower spike, which turns in a slight spiral. It is dispersed across all continents, many species being simply extreme variations of one parent species. This species, from the east coast of the United States and Canada, is both terrestrial and aquatic. It flourishes almost everywhere, growing as happily along roadsides as in very open undergrowth or in marshland, where it is almost aquatic. It is an undemanding plant, and flowers in spring and autumn in an intermediate house.

Right

Staurochilus fasciatus (×2.7)

The name of the genus comes from the Greek *stauros* (cross) and *keilos* (lip), owing to its cross-shaped labellum. It is often confused with the genus *Trichoglottis*. It consists of four East Asian species, this being the most representative. It is a hot-house plant, flowering in April and May.

Stenoglottis longifolia (× 0.95)

This African genus comprises both terrestrial plants and epiphytes. This example is terrestrial, robust and vigorous, and very easy to propagate by root division. In a cool house, it needs plenty of light, and should be kept dry in winter. It is repotted at the end of March–April, and flowers from September to December.

Right
Trichoceros parviflorus (×3)

This small genus comes from the Cordilleras of the Andes. This species, resembling a bee, is found in the Tarma region between Palca and Carpapata in Peru, at an altitude of 2,900 m (9,500 ft). It grows on cacti, putting it within easy reach of the bees. It should be cultivated in a small pot or on a slab of cork bark, in a cool house, where it will flower from September to March.

Trigonidium acuminatum (× 3.15)

These are epiphytic plants from tropical America, encountered from Mexico to Brazil. The name comes from the Greek *trigonos* (triangular), a reference to the shape of the flower. This species is grown in a hot to intermediate house, where it flowers in autumn.

Trigonidium egertonianum

(× 4.25)

This native epiphyte of tropical America is found from Mexico to Venezuela. It grows from sea level to an altitude of 1,000 m (3,300 ft), and is cultivated in an intermediate to hot house; avoid excessive watering in winter. It does need a resting period of five weeks if it is to flower well in spring.

Trisetella triglochin (×5.15)

This genus is one of five making up the tribe *Masdevallidae*; its classification was reviewed in 1980 by C.A. Luer. The genus was established by Reichenbach under the name *Triaristella*, which is still found in the literature. This dwarf epiphyte is grown in an intermediate house, and needs to be kept moist all year, except on very cold winter days.

above

Thrixspermum canifledu (× 2.15)

This genus takes its name from the Greek *thrix* (hair) and *sperma* (seed). It is found from Sri Lanka to the Ryuku islands of Japan, and comprises 137 species, all epiphytes of medium size. This one, which is highly representative of the genus, is grown half-shaded in a hot house, and flowers in spring.

Synonym: *Vanda denisoniana* v. *hebraica.* This genus takes its name from the Sanskrit; it is without doubt the genus most represented amongst orchids in cultivation. This hot-house species needs plenty of light. It is grown in a pot, in pine bark, avoiding excessive watering in winter.

Right Vuylstekeara Cambria 'Plush' (×0.75)

This is a multigeneric hybrid genus from *Cochlioda*, *Miltonia*, and *Odontoglossum*, created in 1904 by the greatest Belgian horticulturist of his time, Charles Vuylsteke. This hybrid was raised in 1931 by Charles Worth in England and is, without doubt, the current favourite. It should be grown indoors and kept slightly moist, but never dry, or in an intermediate house, half-shaded. It flowers in spring, and almost all year.

Left Vanda Golamco's Blue Magic 'Aalsmeer Fall' (×0.65)

This is a cross between *Vanda* Gordon Dillon and *Vanda coerulea*. The former is a hybrid created by Boonchoo in Thailand in 1978, from Madame Rattana and Bangkok Blue. *Vandas* are much used in horticulture, and produce many bigeneric hybrids, such as *Vandachnis*, *Vandaenopsis*, and *Vandofinetia*, and multigeneric hybrids, such as *Yusofara*, *Holttumara*, *Lewisara*, and *Devereuxara*. It should be grown in a hot house, where it flowers in autumn.

Facing page Zygopetalum crinitum (×3)

This American genus of epiphytes and terrestrial orchids consists of 20 species, indigenous to southern tropical and subtropical America. This particular species grows in the state of Espírito Santo, Brazil, up to Santa Caterina, and is especially common in the coastal mountains of the Serra da Mantiqueira. It is a protected plant, flowering in November. It should be cultivated in an intermediate to cool house. It is important to suspend watering from the month of August. It should be kept moist, with plenty of light, and full light at the end of September.

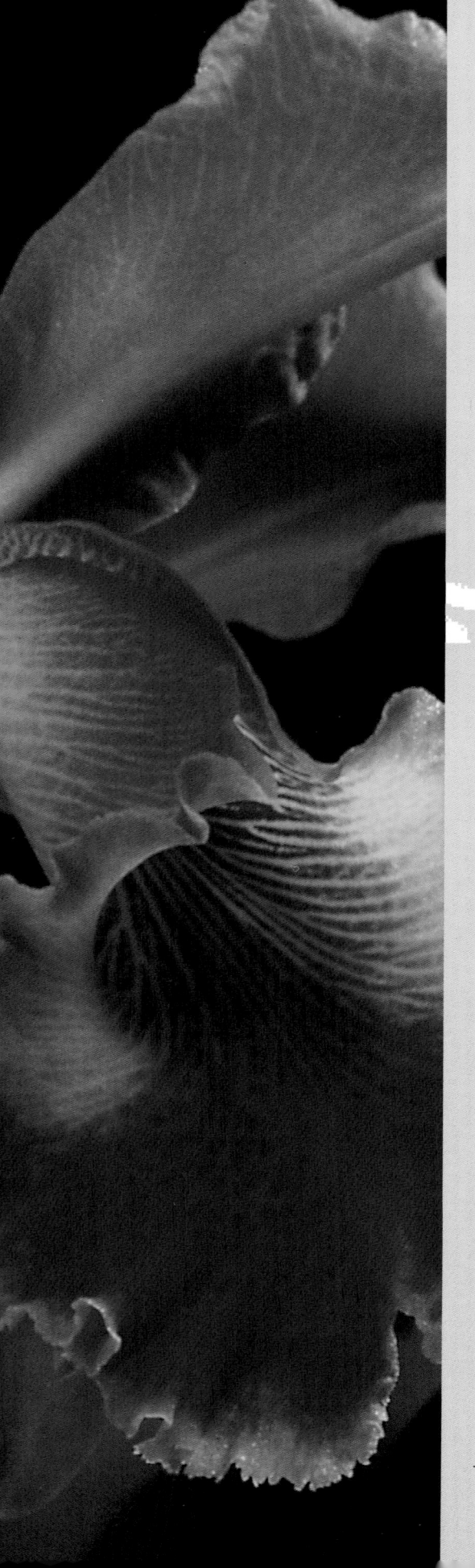

*T*hree centuries of orchid culture have perfected the art to the point where it now lies within everyone's reach. Anyone can choose to own one, several, or even a whole collection of these magnificent plants.

Nevertheless, it is important to obtain information from the seller about the cultural needs of a particular plant before making a final choice. It is vital to know its requirements as to temperature, light, feeding, and so on, in order to judge whether you can provide them. There has been a change in the use of heating over the years. Remember that the warmth of a house will vary according to the level of occupation. It is a wise first step to keep note of the temperature in the spot where you plan to put your plant(s), at various different times of day over a 24 hour period. Only once you have this information will you be able to set out confidently to acquire the orchid of your dreams.

Cultivation

Compost

There have been great changes in recent years in the types of growing medium used for pot culture of these plants. Those most commonly used are pine bark mixed with peat, or a mixture of pine bark, artificial (polyurethane) moss, and peat. The demands of nature conservation mean that the roots of tree ferns or osmunda are no longer used. For the same reasons, peat, which is presently used in horticulture in vast quantities, is certain to be abandoned in the near future. Composted vegetable matter, coconut fibre, and small pieces of cocoa shell, on the other hand, are finding increasing use in orchid compost. A great many Phalaenopsis are now being grown in a coconut–pine bark mixture. Plastic pots are recommended as containers, as they are light, retain the warmth around the roots, and retain moisture better.

Watering

This is difficult to do well; the ability to judge by eye is more important than any hard and fast rule. Orchids need plenty of water during growth, but their roots must never be allowed to remain in water.

If the plant is growing in a pine bark mixture, in a temperature of 18°C (64°F) by night and 21°C (70°F) by day, it will need to be watered twice a week. The following come into this category: Phalaenopsis, Cattleyas, Paphiopedilums of the Maudiae type, Encyclias, Epidendrums, Beallaras, and Ansellias. In a mixture of peat, artificial moss and bark, watering once a week is generally sufficient.

Plants which require a temperature of 15°C (59°F) by night and 20°C (68°F) by day, such as Burragearas, Vuylstek-earas, Oncidiums, Odontocidiums, and Miltoniopsis, also need to be watered once a week. Hot-house Dendrobiums need a great deal of water during development of the pseudobulbs. Watering should then be reduced by half. In winter, they need to be kept slightly moist. The same applies for certain Oncidiums, Brassias, and Encyclias. Indoors, where there is often insufficient humidity, it helps to spray the leaves several times a week. With Phalaenopsis, avoid spraying the centre of the plant.

The method of watering is simple: the plant is placed in a sink, and the water poured onto the pot from above. It is then allowed to drain before being replaced in position.

There would be no sense in discussing watering without mentioning the type of water; this is important for the long-term survival of the plants. Orchids need a fairly neutral, lime-free water (pH 5.8). Ordinary mains water often contains too much lime and chlorine, so it is better to use rainwater. If this is unavailable, water which has been boiled a few days in advance can be used instead.

There are two types of lime, active and otherwise. The active type causes patches to form on the leaves, and slows down photosynthesis. The roots then become wrinkled, and the build-up of lime can eventually prevent photosynthesis altogether.

Never use distilled water, and ensure that the water used is never too cold or too warm.

Humidity

Orchids come from the humid regions of the world. The level of humidity is therefore an important factor when they are being cultivated in an artificial environment.

Indoors, the humidity around the plants usually needs to be 40 – 60 per cent. This can be achieved by filling a tray (like the developing dish used by photographers) with gravel, adding water, putting a grid on top, and placing the pots on this.

In the greenhouse, humidity decreases during the day with the ventilation, and rises again at night. Damping down, by spraying the ground in the greenhouse in the morning, will be necessary, and the leaves too should be sprayed. Some amateurs install a small pump with fixed jets covering the surface of the greenhouse. This system operates on a timer, and is especially useful in hot weather, spraying two or three times a day. Care is needed in judging humidity: cool, damp weather does not necessarily mean high humidity in the greenhouse. It may prove extremely helpful to use a hygrometer.

Ventilation

In their natural environment, most orchids grow at quite a high altitude. Cool-house types will therefore need plenty of fresh air. In an intermediate house, in hot weather, it is best to have some movement of air to prevent fungal attack. The solution is either to open a ventilator when necessary, sited at the top of the greenhouse or below the staging, or to install a fan.

contain the nutrients in the correct proportions. They are dissolved in the water, when watering in the normal way, at a rate of 0.5 to 1 g per litre ($\frac{1}{12}$ to $\frac{1}{6}$ oz per gallon), and applied once a week.

Special methods for epiphytes

Almost all orchids in cultivation are in fact epiphytes, but the term is used loosely here to refer to those plants which are grown on bark (cork or tree fern).

Two or three times a week, the support needs to be watered by dipping it in water or spraying. In spring and summer, this may need to be done every day.

Special conditions for indoor culture

In general, the humidity indoors falls below 30 per cent, there is little movement of air, and light is limited. However, there is no need to be discouraged by these minor problems; they can easily be corrected. All that is needed is to spray every day, and to ventilate the room night and day, weather permitting, or to install a small fan (taking care to avoid draughts).

To increase the light, additional artificial lighting can be provided, even if only for a few hours a day. For this, fluorescent tubes are used, set at least a metre (3 ft) away from the plants. Orchids need at least twelve hours of light per day.

Light

Contrary to common belief, with the exception of a few rare types, cultivated orchids need plenty of light. However, if the light is too intense, the plants yellow and fail to grow. Too much shading, on the other hand, produces limp plants which do not flower. Whether in front of a window or in the greenhouse, direct sunlight should be avoided.

Shading

The white shading used by professionals is not recommended for small, amateur greenhouses. Here, the best solution is to fix shading blinds about 20 cm (7 in) away from the glass, which can be unrolled early in the morning, and rolled up again at night.

Feeding

It was thought for a long time that orchids, being slow-growing, needed little or no feeding. But in fact, like every other plant, they do need feeding during growth. Studies show that feeding should follow an established programme over the year: from 15 February to 15 May, a 28-14-14 feed should be given; from mid-May to August, a 20-20-20 feed; from September to October, a more potash-rich feed such as 7-11-27; and from October to mid-November, 20-20-20. No feed should be given from then until February, especially in the North of Europe, less so in the South. Feeds are numbered according to the proportions of the three main nutrients, N-P-K, that is, nitrogen-phosphorus-potash. Fertilizers rich in nitrogen are recommended for foliage plants. Any commercially available fertilizers are suitable, as long as they are water-soluble and

PARASITES

– When it is too dry, or when there are draughts, tiny but devastating creatures put in their appearance: red spider mite (*Tetranychus urticae*, *Temuipalpus pacificus*, *Brevipalpus obovatus*). The leaves of species with thin foliage, such as Calanthes, Paphiopedilums, Oncidiums, Vuylstekearas, and Phalaenopsis, become silver-grey. They should then be treated with a suitable insecticide.

– Thrips (*Heliothrips haemorrhoidalis*, *Heliothrips femoralis*) are equally tiny and attack young leaves and flowers. Dryness should be avoided, and infestations should be treated with a proprietary product specific for thrips once a week for a month.

– Several types of scale insect can appear on the plants: small ones, like *Diaspis*, which are mainly found on Cattleyas; *Coccus hesperidum*, commonly found on Phalaenopsis; *Pseudococcus adonidum* (mealy bugs), which are mainly seen on Oncidiums, Vuylstekearas, Lycastes and others. To these we might add *Saissetia hemisohaerica*, with its shell-like covering, which attaches itself to the stems of Lycastes, Odontoglossums and even Phalaenopsis. These will require the use of a proprietary treatment for scale.

– Aphids attack young growth and flower buds, which become deformed and die. These insects also transmit viral diseases. The best treatment indoors is simply to turn the plant upside-down and wash it under lukewarm water from a running tap. In the greenhouse, a pyrethrum-based product can be used.

– The presence of slugs and snails is betrayed by their slimy trails, and by gashes in the leaves and flower buds which they have attacked. A proprietary treatment for slugs will then have to be used.

FUNGAL DISEASES

Fungal infections represent a serious problem for orchids. They gain the upper hand when the humidity gets too high.

– *Phythium ultimum* attacks pseudobulbs and leaves, which then blacken.

– *Fusarium oxysporum* attacks the roots, causing the plant to dry out. There is significant risk of infection when repotting.

Our precious plants are unfortunately subject to attack by many other fungi. Treatment with a proprietary fungicide will be needed, and may sometimes be necessary as a preventive measure against Phalaenopsis.

BACTERIAL DISEASES

These also appear when the humidity is too high. They cause rotting on the leaves, especially of Phalaenopsis and Paphiopedilums.

Bactericidal products do exist, but the most important thing to do, in the case of both bacterial and fungal attack, is to observe some basic rules of hygiene: clean tools, storage of composts in a well-ventilated place, and so on.

VIRUSES

The presence of viruses cannot always be clearly detected; sometimes it is better to go to a specialist for a diagnosis. Mosaic virus produces spotting or marbling on the leaves and flowers. Unfortunately, there is no remedy. The sick plant must be burnt, to prevent contamination of other plants, and more rigorous standards of hygiene must be maintained (in particular, disinfection of the knife or secateurs with a trisodium solution, or by passing the blade through a flame). It should be remembered that viruses can also be passed on by insects (aphids, thrips, etc.).

Do not be discouraged by this catalogue of disasters, or by the various growing conditions required. Most common orchids are easy to care for. On the whole they thrive, and soon outgrow their pots. You may find yourself having to move house!

Repotting

This is generally carried out every three years, so as not to disturb the plant unnecessarily. Repotting is done in spring for plants which flower in autumn, and in September–October for those flowering in spring. The plant is removed from its old pot, and any black or soft roots are cut away. If necessary, the back-bulb is also cut off. The old compost is removed. To repot orchids which form pseudobulbs, place the pseudobulb against the edge of the pot, so that the new growth is positioned somewhere around the middle of the pot. To repot orchids which do not form pseudobulbs, such as Phalaenopsis, for example, position the plant in the middle of the pot. Fill in with compost, pressing firmly (unless bark is being used). It should be kept moist, but not wet. Regular watering is resumed after four weeks.

The plants which we cultivate come from regions of the globe where days and nights are of equal length. Our familiar seasons are replaced by a wet season and a dry season. At higher altitudes, there is a great deal of rain. At lower levels, humidity is very high, and rain mainly falls at night. The following calendar is based on a century of horticultural experience. The temperatures given are minimum ones; you may exceed them, but do not drop below the recommended limit.

JANUARY

During the winter months, artificial heating is necessary, to warm and also to purify the air in a greenhouse. There are three types of greenhouse:
– hot house: the daytime temperature here is between 20 and 25°C (68 and 77°F). At night, it is 18°C (64°F). Humidity is low or stable.
– intermediate house: the daytime temperature is between 14 and 18°C (57 and 64°F), with 14°C (57°F) at night. Humidity is low or stable.
– cool house: the temperature ranges between 9 and 12°C (48 and 54°F) during the day, and is 8°C (46°F) at night. Humidity will be rising or stable.
– *Cattleya, Brassocattleya, Brassolaeliocattleya, Sophrolaeliocattleya, Laeliocattleya, Potinara* and *Laeliocatonia*: be careful with watering. The plants should be kept slightly moist, with no spraying of the foliage. Excessively low temperatures should be avoided. The minimum temperatures generally mark a definite lower limit, and it is important not to go below these; otherwise there is a risk of spots forming on the leaves.
– *Cymbidium*: the night-time temperature should not be allowed to fall below 12°C (54°F). White-flowered species of *Cymbidium* are more fragile than others. Development of the flower spikes occurs at around 15°C (59°F). Do not spray flowers or foliage. Water in moderation. Fertilizer can be given at a rate of 0.5 g per litre ($^1/_{12}$ oz per gallon) of water. *Cymbidium devonianum* should be hung as near to the light as possible.
– *Paphiopedilum*: this is the month when many flower, or are in bud. It is better to delay repotting until February. If you have already repotted them, it helps to raise the temperatures. Keep the plants moist, and maintain humidity by a light damping down.
– *Phalaenopsis*: a few may suspend all growth. It helps to produce a fine plant if the temperature is kept at 20°C (68°F), and good air circulation maintained. *Fusarium* (a fungus) and bacteria are active at low temperatures. Plants should be watered once a week, at the same time as feeding, at a rate of 0.5 g of fertilizer per litre ($^1/_{12}$ oz per gallon) of water.
– Hot-house Dendrobiums: give very little water, just enough to keep the roots moist. Red spider mite is often found on these plants, and should be treated.
– Various: *Coelogyne cristata, Coelogyne ochracea*, and all orchids from the Indies which are grown in the cool house, should be kept slightly moist and in full light. *Pleione*: dry; *Dendrobium nobile*: six weeks' suspension of watering, during which cool conditions are needed (around 10°C, or 50°F). *Dendrobium pierardii, Dendrobium aggregatum*, and *Dendrobium densiflorum*, in the intermediate house, need little watering. The Australian Dendrobiums, such as *Dendrobium kingianum, Dendrobium speciosum* and *Dendrobium delicatum*, should be placed in full light (dry side).

FEBRUARY

This midwinter month is much the same as the previous one. However, the days begin to draw out again, and the light gets stronger.

– *Cattleya*: these should not be repotted yet, but with this in mind, watering with a nitrogenous fertilizer should be started with a composition of 28-14-14, at 0.5 g per litre ($^1/_{12}$ oz per gallon) of water. The rate of 1 g per litre ($^1/_6$ oz per gallon) must not be exceeded.

– Miniature Cymbidiums will be in full flower. On no account should there be any spraying. Concentrate instead on watering, once a week or every ten days, according to the weather. A 28-14-14 fertilizer can be added at a rate of 0.75 g per litre ($^1/_{10}$ oz per gallon). Watch out for slugs. Ventilate, if the weather is good.

– *Paphiopedilum*: repotting. If any are affected by *Fusarium* or *Phytophtora*, the compost should be removed, the old roots cut away, and the plant cleaned and dipped in a solution of Fongaride WP 25. Before repotting, the plants should be kept moist, but not wet. Supply fertilizer at a rate of 0.5 g per litre ($^1/_{12}$ oz per gallon) of water.

– *Phalaenopsis*: water in moderation, avoiding wetting the centre of the plant. In the case of *Phalaenopsis*, plants affected by fungus are treated with Fongaride WP 25, at a rate of 2 g per litre ($^1/_3$ oz per gallon) of water; if there are black spots, use Zinebe: 3 g per litre ($^1/_2$ oz per gallon) of water. Another cause of black spots, *Phythium*, can arise when either the water or the air is too cold or the air circulation poor. Details like these will need to be checked.

– *Dendrobium*: The buds on *Dendrobium nobile* will be starting to form. It should now be kept warmer. Full light. Water in moderation.

– Various: Encyclias, *Brassia verrucosa*, *Lycaste cruenta*, and *Lycaste aromatica*

should be given only very little water. *Lycaste skinneri*: keep moist. *Miltonia*, *Miltoniopsis*: water in moderation, once every ten days. *Dendrobium pierardii*, *Dendrobium transparens*: the buds will be starting to form; water twice a week. *Dendrobium thyrsiflorum* and *Dendrobium formosum* will still be in the resting stage. Keep dry. *Rossioglossum*: slightly moist. *Coelogyne cristata*, in the cool house, will be forming its buds; water once a week. *Cattleya forbesii*, *Cattleya intermedia* and *Ansellia africana*: water in moderation. *Vanda*: water well, once a week; no spraying of the leaves, or only in fine sunny weather. *Phaius*: water once a week. *Zygopetalum*, *Calanthe masuca*: repot. Plants mounted on bark can be given more water, except for Encyclias and Dendrobiums, which are still in the resting stage. The miniature Central American orchids are to be kept slightly moist. Neofinetias and Aerides should be well watered. Calanthes, Cycnoches, Catasetums and Mormodes are still dormant. Care of African species depends on the weather. Sunny and dry: a little water. Damp and cold: it is better to keep them dry. In the hot house: a little more humidity. *Angraecum*: avoid spraying the leaves. *Oncidium*: water well. *Dendrobium*: water simply to prevent the plant from becoming wrinkled.

MARCH

In the greenhouse, this marks the beginning of the year's growth.

In the hot house: temperatures are rising. Ventilate when they climb above 25°C (77°F). The minimum at night is 18°C (64°F). The humidity should be progressively increased.

In the intermediate house: daytime temperature of 18 to 20°C (64 to 68°F); at night, 16°C (61°F). The humidity should gradually be increased.

In the cool house: the temperature

remains between 12 and 16°C (54 and 61°F). Ventilate if it rises above 18°C (64°F). At night, it drops to about 9°C (48°F) and the humidity also increases. In some regions, the sun can become strong, so shading is important, using either blinds or a white shading wash on the glass. Ventilate according to the weather. Indoors, direct sunlight should be avoided.

– Cattleyas which flowered in the autumn are repotted if necessary. If the compost is based on pine bark, plants should be watered once a week; for a peat-based compost, only once a fortnight. Fertilizer: 0.75 g per litre ($^1/_{10}$ oz per gallon) of water. Watch out for slugs.

– *Cymbidium*: flowering is at its peak. Plants which have finished flowering can be repotted if required. If necessary, night-time temperatures should be maintained at 15°C (59°F). Do not shade. Ventilate as much as possible when the weather is good. Red spider mite may attack your plants. Treat with a solution of Pentac, 1 g per litre ($^1/_6$ oz per gallon) of water and repeat the treatment a fortnight later. Fertilizer: 28-14-14, at 1 g per litre ($^1/_6$ oz per gallon) of water; water well.

– *Paphiopedilum*: shade well (50 per cent). Water only if the plant is dry. Fertilizer: 28-14-14, at 0.5 g per litre ($^1/_{12}$ oz per gallon) of water. All the plants which require it should be repotted. Check for slugs, and use slug pellets.

– *Phalaenopsis*: shade well. Maintain good humidity in the greenhouse, ventilating only in hot weather above 25°C (77°F). Fertilizer: 0.75 g per litre ($^1/_{10}$ oz per gallon) of water. Water once a week.

– *Calanthe*: if the new shoot on *Calanthe vestita* reaches a length of 5 cm (2 in), repot. Give plenty of light. In a hot house or sunny room, keep the plant moist.

– *Odontoglossum*: also related species: shade well, and ventilate even at night, weather permitting. Watering: add 28-14-14 fertilizer at 0.75 g per litre ($^1/_{10}$ oz per gallon) of water. Water once every ten days. Repot Rossioglossums and all the Odontoglossums which flowered in the autumn. Do not spray excessively.

– *Oncidium*: *Oncidium varicosum* should now be given more water and fertilizer. *Oncidium ornithorhynchum* needs repotting. *Oncidium leucochilum* is forming flower spikes. Take care not to over-water *Oncidium cebolleta* and *Oncidium sprucei*. Full light.

– Various: *Brassia*: all species should now be kept slightly moist. *Coelogyne cristata*: moisten thoroughly. *Anguloa*: still dry (but not dried out). *Miltonia* and *Miltoniopsis*: shade well. All miniatures should have 50 per cent light. Red spider mite and slugs need controlling. Catasetums, Lycastes, Peristerias, Mormodes, and Zygopetalums should be repotted. Avoid spraying the new growth.

APRIL

This is the month of rebirth. The temperatures given here are those to be maintained when the sky is overcast. In sunny weather, they will increase by themselves.

In the hot house: a daytime temperature of 20 to 25°C (68 to 77°F); 18°C (64°F) at night. Increase humidity.

In the intermediate house: 18 to 20°C (64 to 68°F) by day; 16°C (61°F) by night. Increase humidity.

In the cool house: 15 to 16°C (59 to 61°F) by day; 11°C (52°F) by night. Increase humidity. Take care: shading should be in place all season.

– *Cattleya*: water using a nitrogenous fertilizer on the basis of 0.5 g per litre ($^1/_{12}$ oz per gallon) of water. Repotting should be done now, followed by copious watering. After three weeks, water

normally. Repot those plants which have a shoot 5 cm (2 in) long. The roots develop more quickly.

This is the month for repotting hothouse Dendrobiums. Repotting every two years is sufficient. Do not use too big a pot; just one which is 2 cm ($^1/_{10}$ in) bigger than the plant. Keep warm, slightly moist, spray if the weather allows, and shade no more than a little.

– *Cymbidium*: water every fortnight with a 28-14-14 fertilizer. Ventilate well. If you live in a region where the cold weather is already over, and all risk of frost is past, Cymbidiums can be placed outside, half-shaded, at the end of the month. *Cymbidium lowianum* is still in flower.

– *Paphiopedilums*: if grown in a greenhouse or in their own separate area, ventilate in moderation. Maintain humidity, shade well, and avoid prolonged damping down.

– *Odontoglossum, Miltoniopsis*: keep a careful watch on the temperature. Shade well. Water between once and twice a week with a 28-14-14 fertilizer made up at a rate of 0.5 g per litre ($^1/_{12}$ oz per gallon) of water.

– *Phalaenopsis*: shade well. Feed with nitrogenous fertilizer added at a rate of 0.75 g per litre ($^1/_{10}$ oz per gallon) of water. If flowering is over, maintain a night-time temperature of 16°C (61°F) for six weeks.

– Various: many genera are in bud, others are in flower. The most important tasks are repotting and cleaning, along with watering. If you have not yet repotted Cycnoches, Mormodes, and Catasetums, do this now. Damping down should preferably be done in the morning. All plants which have ended their resting period should be repotted, if necessary. Water with a nitrogenous fertilizer a fortnight after repotting.

MAY

From 15 May, the temperatures are readjusted. Some plants are outside in the garden, half-shaded. These should be watered, with feed, once a week, even if it has rained.

In the hot house: temperature 18 to 22°C (64 to 72°F) by day; 18°C (64°F) by night. Humidity increasing.

In the intermediate house: 20°C (68°F) by day; 16°C (61°F) by night. Increase humidity.

In the cool house: 11 to 16°C (52 to 61°F) by day; 11°C (52°F) by night.

– Cattleya: only those which flowered during the winter need repotting; Cattleya is repotted every two or three years. Water once a week. These plants should not be put into the garden; they must be cultivated in the greenhouse. Continue to water with a nitrogenous fertilizer.

– Cymbidium: repotting is in full swing. The pot should be a fair size, but not too big. The plant will be growing in it for three or four years, even if the pseudobulbs spill over. Water with a 20-20-20 fertilizer, made up using 1 g per litre ($^1/_6$ oz per gallon) of water. Stop all nitrogen-rich fertilizers.

– Paphiopedilum: shade is important. A good damping down is needed in the morning, depending on the weather. Ventilate more in the evening than during the day. Check the compost before watering. Give 20-20-20 fertilizer, made up using 0.5 g per litre ($^1/_{12}$ oz per gallon) of water.

– Phalaenopsis: keep moist, but avoid spraying too much water into the centre of the plant. Maintain the heating at night, if necessary. Shade well and ventilate. Avoid low temperatures, which produce condensation and so encourage Botrytis to form on the flowers. Continue watering with 20-20-20 fertilizer made up using 0.5 g per litre ($^1/_{12}$ oz per gallon) of water.

– Hot-house Dendrobiums can still be repotted if you have not already done this. Give as much light as possible. Fertilizer may be applied to plants which have not been repotted, at 1 g per litre ($^1/_6$ oz per gallon) of water.

– Odontoglossums, Lemboglossum bictoniense, and Rossioglossums can be put into the garden, half-shaded, if you live in a region where the hot weather has already arrived. They are sensitive to excessive heat, but must not be exposed to any chill, so do not put them out unless the weather is appropriate. Ventilate well and maintain humidity both in the greenhouse and indoors.

JUNE

This is the month of the longest days, when the warmth of summer should benefit the plants. Full attention must be given to ventilation and watering. If the nights are cool, maintain the heating in the hot house. Water clay pots more generously, as a rule, once every three days; plastic pots need watering only once a week. Water plants mounted on slabs of cork bark or tree fern every other day.

If the heating is no longer needed, it is enough to water once a week, especially for plants mounted on tree fern slabs. Fertilizer with a 20-20-20 composition is applied at 0.75 g per litre ($^1/_{10}$ oz per gallon) of water. Ventilate every day, except when the weather is overcast, especially if it is raining. Paphiopedilums grown in the greenhouse are ventilated less by day and more by night, especially in regions where they experience dryness. All the orchids must be shaded except Cymbidiums.

If there is a heatwave outside, however, it is wise to shade the Cymbidiums too. If you have only one or two plants, it would be best to put them in the garden, half-shaded, and water them well. Daytime temperatures outside will generally be higher than those required in the greenhouse. Experience often shows that the temperatures fall into two types, one occurring when the sun is high, and the other in stormy weather. When the sun disappears, the temperature falls. In Northern regions of Europe, nights remain very cool. Keep a careful watch on the humidity if you are not using heating at night.

– Cattleya: if you have to repot these, now is the time to do so. Water and feed once a week; 50 per cent shade.

– Cymbidium: these were repotted or divided in May. No more repotting should be done until September. Ventilate whenever possible, day and night. Water and feed with 20-20-20 fertilizer, 1 g per litre ($^1/_6$ oz per gallon) of water, once a week. Watch for red spider mite.

– Paphiopedilum: if these are the only plants in the greenhouse, ventilate in hot weather, especially at night, so as to avoid loss of humidity. Give 20-20-20 fertilizer, 0.5 g per litre ($^1/_{12}$ oz per gallon) of water. Shade well.

– Phalaenopsis: during this period when the heating is used little, if at all, water carefully and very early in the morning, to give the plant time to become dry by evening. Too much water on the leaves triggers a type of rot known as Erwinia. Good circulation of air is helpful. Fertilizer: 20-20-20, 0.5 g per litre ($^1/_{12}$ oz per gallon) of water.

– Calanthe: growth is strong, and requires 20-20-20 fertilizer, 1 g per litre ($^1/_6$ oz per gallon) of water.

– Odontoglossum and Miltonia: in summer, Odontoglossum crispum suffers from the heat. Damp down by spraying the floor of the greenhouse thoroughly to maintain humidity, and spray the foliage lightly in the morning. Shading is needed, to keep the temperature down. (The same goes for Miltoniopsis, which are generally sensitive to high temperatures.)

Miltonia clowesii, Miltonia regnelli, Miltonia cruenta, and Miltonia Moir are species from Brazil. They need more light and warmth than the others. Water in accordance with the weather.

July

Midsummer marks the middle of the year, and of the summer season, but from then on, the days will shorten. Nights may still be cool in some regions.

In the hot house: maintain temperatures of 22°C (72°F) by night and 27°C (81°F) by day, as well as high humidity.

In the intermediate house: 25°C (77°F) by day; 18°C (64°F) by night.

In the cool house: a difficult month. Shade well. Daytime temperature, 18°C (64°F); by night, 12°C (54°F) with sustained humidity. Ventilate day and night.

In this month, watering and damping down are the most important tasks. Rainwater is recommended. Tap water is only used for damping down the floor of the greenhouse. If the weather is fine, and temperatures high, damp down in the morning and towards the end of the afternoon. Ventilate every day. Be on the watch for thunderstorms, and close the ventilators when it rains. At any time of year, you should look out for changes of weather. Ventilators need to be closed before the rain comes in! Open ventilators on the side away from the wind. Close ventilators at night in the hot house. Use shading everywhere. Only in the case of Cymbidiums use light shading.

– *Phalaenopsis, Paphiopedilum, Cattleya*: shade, and continue to water with a 20-20-20 fertilizer, 0.75 g per litre (1/10 oz per gallon) of water.

– *Dendrobium nobile, Zygopetalum* and *Paphiopedilum insigne*: all watering with

a feed should be stopped. Be vigilant and treat for red spider mite and thrips.

August

Towards the end of the month, extremely hot weather is less frequent.

In the hot house: daytime temperature between 23 and 27°C (73 to 81°F); 21°C (70°F) by night. Maintain the humidity.

In the intermediate house: 21 to 23°C (70 to 73°F) by day; 18°C (64°F) by night.

In the cool house: 16 to 18°C (61 to 64°F) by day; 12°C (54°F) by night. Maintain the humidity. Ventilate night and day.

– *Cattleya*: all the shoots will have developed on some, in anticipation of flowering. Give a potash-rich feed, at 0.5 g per litre (1/12 oz per gallon) of water. *Cattleya labiata* and *Cattleya bowringiana* receive more light at the end of the month. Take care if the month of August proves humid, and avoid damping down in the intermediate house in the late afternoon. Indoors, continue to spray once a week. Give plenty of light. In the greenhouse, water according to the night-time temperature inside. If no heating is being used, you will need a fan to keep the air inside the greenhouse sweet; there will otherwise be a dank smell. Use a potash-rich fertilizer, at 0.5 g per litre (1/12 oz per gallon) of water.

– *Paphiopedilum*: stop feeding. Water once a week; spray the foliage in the morning, when it is hot. *Paphiopedilum St Albans*, *Paphiopedilum Pinocchio*, and *Paphiopedilum haynaldianum* will be in flower.

– *Odontoglossum*: damp down in between the pots. Ventilate well at night.

– *Miltoniopsis*: avoid excessive heat; shade well; indoors, spray for humidity every day. Apply fertilizer once a week. In the greenhouse, ventilation and humidity are essential. If there are black spots on the leaves, treat with Zinebe at 0.6 g per litre ($1/11$ oz per gallon) of water. Watch for red spider mite, which produces a silvery appearance on the underside of the leaves. Treat with Pentac, 1 g per litre ($1/6$ oz per gallon) of water.

– *Rossioglossum grande* will flower at the end of the month. *Rossioglossum schlieperianum* is in flower.

SEPTEMBER

The days are shortening, and the nights becoming cool. Additional heating will be needed in rainy weather. If you are using roller blinds for shading, and if your greenhouse is so oriented, remove the shading on the north side. The temperatures are as for August. Take care, because the cool nights will lead to a great deal of humidity. Stop damping down underneath the staging. If you have plants outside, it is wise to bring them back in, and give them maximum light. Temperature: 17°C (63°F). Combat slugs, which are starting to become active.

– *Paphiopedilum*: keep moist. Maintain shading. No fertilizer.

– *Odontoglossum crispum* and *Miltoniopsis*: now that the summer heat has abated, you can repot those plants which need it. If *Lemboglossum bictoniense* has been in the garden, it should be brought back into the greenhouse or indoors. Water in moderation.

– *Phalaenopsis*: any repotting should be done now. Keep the plants moist and shaded afterwards. If you are using clay pots, water around the pots.

– Hot-house *Dendrobiums* have matured, and are forming their flower buds. Keep the pots moist, but not wet. Give maximum light.

– *Dendrobium nobile*: full light; no fertilizer.

– Various: the African orchids are about to flower. Water the cork bark every three days. Daytime temperature 25°C (77°F); 15°C (59°F) by night. *Oncidium varicosum* and hybrids will be in bud.

– *Vanda coerulea* and hybrids: full light. Water once a week. Slugs and red spider mite remain a problem. If roots are in a poor state owing to excessive watering, treat with Fongaride 25 WP.

OCTOBER

This is the month which brings much rain, and a weakening sun; the heating is again needed.

In the hot house: Daytime temperature 21 to 25°C (70 to 77°F). By night, 18°C (64°F), but to combat humidity, it is sometimes necessary to increase to 20°C (68°F), or to use a fan.

In the intermediate house: 18 to 21°C (64 to 70°F) by day; 16°C (61°F) by night. Bring humidity down.

In the cool house: 12°C (54°F) by day; 10°C (50°F) by night. Use a fan to reduce the humidity.

– *Cattleya*: the days ahead will be dark. Water according to the weather, once every ten days. Stop damping down the greenhouse floor and the foliage. Ventilate if the weather is fine. If you do spray foliage for humidity, switch on the fan. Indoors, conditions are different; domestic heating dries the air, so it is helpful to give the plant some humidity. Give 20-20-20 fertilizer, at 0.5 g per litre ($1/12$ oz per gallon) of water.

– *Cymbidium*: this is the month which brings the rewards. The flower spikes are visible. Keep moist, but not to excess. Expose to full light. Water with 20-20-20 fertilizer, using 0.75 g per litre ($1/10$ oz per gallon) of water. Watch for slugs.

– *Paphiopedilum*: many plants are in flower. If they are being grown in the hot house, keep very moist. Intermediate house: fairly moist. Cool house: slightly moist. Take care not to damp down too much. If you have trouble with buds rotting, treat with Zinebe, 3 g per litre ($1/2$ oz per gallon) of water. Maintain good air circulation. Watch for slugs.

– *Phalaenopsis*: the plants repotted in August–September will now have good roots. Water with 20-20-20 fertilizer, 0.75 g per litre ($1/10$ oz per gallon) of water. By the end of the month, shading is no longer necessary.

– *Calanthe*: the *vestita* type will be in bud, or almost in flower. Reduce watering to once a fortnight. The leaves will now be turning yellowish-brown. They should be cut off with a knife, but not until they have turned completely brown, so as to avoid infection.

– Various: most species are mature. Continue to water in moderation. If you have a greenhouse divided into three sections, transfer *Dendrobium nobile* to the cool house. Continue to water Lycastes, but stop watering Catasetums, Mormodes, and Cycnoches. Watch for slugs.

NOVEMBER

This is one of the darkest months of the year. Check the heating carefully.

In the hot house: the temperature by day should be 20 to 22°C (68 to 72°F); by night, 18°C (64°F). Humidity should be low.

In the intermediate house: 18°C (64°F) by day; 15°C (59°F) by night. Humidity low.

In the cool house: 12°C (54°F) by day, 9°C (48°F) by night. Humidity low.

This is the time to clean and weed the staging and the pots. Renew the plastic covering the inside of the greenhouse, and clean the glass, so as to admit as much light as possible. Stop damping down the plants, but maintain the humidity under the staging, if necessary.

Indoors, prepare the plants for winter. Change the gravel in the saucers. Do not repot any plants until spring.

– *Cattleya*: the tasks are as for October. Plants which are still developing a pseudobulb should be given full light to ripen them, until they flower in January–February. The others should now be kept slightly moist, just enough to prevent drying out of the pseudobulbs. If you are maintaining the minimum temperatures, avoid frequent damping down or watering. At high temperatures, on the other hand, water every week.

– *Cymbidium*: the task here is to support the flower spikes. Watch for slugs.

– *Paphiopedilum*: remove all shading. Water in moderation, without letting the plants become dry. Stop damping down.

– *Phalaenopsis*: shading is no longer necessary. Many *Phalaenopsis* are starting to form one or more flowers; *Phalaenopsis speciosa* v. *tetraspis* will have flowered. Water in the morning, once a week. Take care, when doing so, not to wet the foliage too much.

– Various: give full light to Odontoglossums, in the cool house. If the daytime temperature rises above 15°C (59°F), ventilate. Miltonias from Brazil need placing in the intermediate house. *Coelogyne cristata* and Dendrobiums from Australia should be watered once every ten days, depending on the weather outside. The hot-house *Dendrobium superbum* hybrids are now kept slightly moist. Hot-house Oncidiums on which a shoot is forming are watered normally. Avoid watering the shoot. Mormodes, Catasetums, and Cycnoches should be kept dry and in the light. *Encyclia*: water once a fortnight.

Epidendrums should be developing a flower spike which will flower in the spring. Water once a week. In the intermediate house, Sobralias and Bulbophyllums should be kept very moist. *Dendrobium thyrsiflorum*, *Dendrobium densiflorum*, *Dendrobium farmeri*, and *Dendrobium anosmum* must stay slightly moist. If there are black spots on the leaves, these are probably caused by poor air circulation. Treat with Zinebe or Eupareen.

Artificial lighting may be used during this month to provide additional light. Do not use this for more than 12 hours a day.

December

In the hot house: daytime temperature: 20 to 25°C (68 to 77°F); by night, 18°C (64°F). Humidity declining.

In the intermediate house: 16 to 18°C (61 to 64°F) by day; 15°C (59°F) by night. Humidity declining.

In the cool house: 10 to 13°C (50 to 55°F) by day; 8°C (46°F) by night. Humidity stable. December is the month which brings the rewards; many orchids are in flower. Winter often causes problems for many amateurs. Artificial heating is in constant use, and dries the air inside. This lack of humidity can be treated by spraying the ground inside the greenhouse. Cold water must not be used on the plants in winter. They need to be given their moisture in moderation, as the roots are very sensitive both to dryness and to excessive wetness. The pseudobulbs must not become wrinkled. Good air circulation produces a good atmosphere, but the orientation of the greenhouse is another factor in deciding how to water or damp down. These remarks are just as appropriate to indoor culture. Never ventilate when the weather is cold.

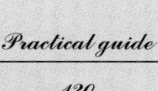

– *Cattleya*: as for November.

– *Cymbidium*: maintain a temperature of 15°C (59°F). A temperature which is either too high or too low causes buds to yellow and fall off. Mice are the enemies of these plants; they take the pollen from the flowers.

– *Paphiopedilum*: these are in bud, or in flower. Keep slightly moist. Do not spray.

– *Phalaenopsis*: the focus of attention must be the temperature of the greenhouse or room. The temperatures given here are minima, which must be respected. Water every week; if growing in clay pots, once every four days. Always water in the morning. Do not water in rainy or misty weather.

– Various: *Dendrobium superbum* will have finished flowering in the hot house, as will the *Dendrobium biggibum* hybrids. If they are still in bud, these will probably now yellow; lack of light and air pollution are the causes. If you have a greenhouse with three sections, transfer *Dendrobium nobile* to the cool house for five weeks, to promote bud formation. *Oncidium splendidum* is forming its flower spikes and needs to be kept dry, with plenty of light. *Coelogyne cristata*, *Coelogyne corymbosa*, *Coelogyne barbata*, *Coelogyne flaccida*, and *Coelogyne ochracea*, which flower in late February–March, should now be kept slightly moist. Watch for red spider mite, both in the greenhouse and indoors.

How to propagate orchids

PROPAGATION BY SEED

In the early days of orchid cultivation, the sowing of seed was a delicate problem, which did not always lead to the hoped-for results. The seeds were sown next to the adult plant, in the expectation that they would soon germinate. Then, in 1899, Noël Bernard discovered that germination required the presence of a fungus. In those days, orchid-growers grew mycelium in tubes, and then transferred it to other tubes containing the seed. This somewhat inefficient method was superseded by a new procedure described by Dr Knudson in a lecture to the Sorbonne in 1920. He demonstrated the germination of orchid seeds in an agar jelly medium without the fungus, using mineral salts, and the addition of 2 per cent sugar. In France, his lecture sent shockwaves through specialist circles. The scientific community refused to acknowledge the facts.

Today, this seed-sowing technique has been perfected, and can be used by amateurs. Completely sterile sowing is possible with ready-to-use, commercially prepared dishes of nutrient jelly, and sterile cabins large enough for one or even two people. Pyrex flasks are no longer required. Irradiated plastic dishes are filled with agar, and the orchid seeds injected into the jelly through a syringe.

However, it is worth mentioning that the natural method of raising from seed is still used by a small group of orchid-growers who wish to perpetuate the tradition. The Japanese *Calanthe* society has a rule obliging its members to sow *Calanthe* seeds (native to Japan) without artificial aid.

VEGETATIVE PROPAGATION

Orchids, like all the higher plants, can be propagated by division. This is the simplest way to produce new plants for a collection. It would be wrong to expect them to be in glorious flower by the following year. This can take several years. Division will produce flowers more quickly than raising from seed, but still takes at least five or six years.

Certain plants, like Dendrobiums, produce *keikis* (Hawaiian for babies) instead of flowers, but in the same position. These are new shoots, which can be potted up once they have formed roots. *Epidendrum ibaguense*, *Epidendrum cinnabarinum* and *Epidendrum secundum* produce shoots on stems that have finished flowering. If the pseudobulbs are separated at the base, and each planted out in a pot, then each will produce a shoot, which takes eighteen months to reach the flowering stage.

After repotting, the back-bulbs which have been removed are kept, and these too can develop shoots. *Coelogyne parishii* and *Coelogyne pandurata* are vigorous, and easily produce several plants in two years. Bulbophyllums are prolific in their production of pseudobulbs, and can be divided before each repotting.

Vandas are monopodial orchids, which can be cut below a set of adventitious* roots when the plant becomes too long, and the section potted up.

Certain Phalaenopsis produce a rosette of leaves on the parent plant. *Pleione formosana* produces bulbils*, which are planted up in a tray in winter. In the greenhouse, *Spathoglottis plicata* and *Cynorkis anacamptoides* produce numerous seeds by self-pollination, which germinate in all the pots in the greenhouse. The roots of *Phalaenopsis stuartiana*, firmly attached to the staging, develop new plantlets, which are potted up into small pots. There are many ways in which we can propagate a plant. Let us not lose sight of the fact, though, that it is in cultivating fine, large specimens that the amateur will find the greatest satisfaction.

Glossary

Adventitious: occurring sporadically or in an unusual place.

Back-bulb: old pseudobulb, as opposed to the one formed in the current year.

Bigeneric: a bigeneric hybrid is the result of a cross between species belonging to two different genera.

Bulbils: small bulbs which form near flowers, or along the edges of leaves.

Caudicle: very small stalk of pollinia.

Column: central, column-shaped organ of orchid flower, formed by the fusing together of stamens and pistil.

Epiphyte: a plant which lives on another plant.

Flower spike: long stem with no leaves, arising from the base, and bearing the flowers.

Genus: (plural: genera). Subdivision of a family, which groups together closely related species. The genus is the first of the two Latin names of a plant. (The second is the species.)

Labellum: one of the three petals of the orchid flower. It differs from the others in shape, size, colour, etc.

Lithophyte: plant which grows on a rock.

Monopodial: monopodial orchids develop from a single main stem; they grow at the extremity of this stem, in an upward direction.

Morphological: relating to its form. Morphology is the study of the form of animals and plants, and of what influences their form.

Multigeneric: A multigeneric hybrid is the result of a cross between species belonging to more than two different genera.

Pollinia: grains of pollen adhering together to form small waxy (not powdery) masses, more or less spherical in shape.

Pseudobulb: a swollen stem, similar in shape to a bulb.

Rhizome: a normally subterranean stem, which grows horizontally. It puts out upward-growing shoots and downward-growing roots. In orchids, it is sometimes subterranean, but more often runs along the surface of the support on which the plant is growing.

Saprophytic: a saprophyte is a plant which lives off dead organisms.

Self-pollination: a flower undergoes self-pollination when its own pollen is deposited on its stigma. The resulting seeds normally exhibit less adaptation than if fertilization involves a cross between two individuals. This is why there are usually mechanisms which prevent self-fertilization. Nevertheless, there are times when one's own seeds are better than no seeds at all.

Stigma: upper part of the pistil (female organ of a flower), onto which the pollen is deposited, so that fertilization can occur.

Sympodial: sympodial orchids form shoots which develop alongside the old shoots, rather than at the end of these. Therefore, as the plant increases in size, it spreads horizontally.

Bibliography

ARDITTI, JOSEPH, *Orchid biology: Reviews and Perspectives II*, Cornell University Press, 1982.

BIRK, LANCE A., *The Paphiopedilum Growers' Manual*, Pisang Press, Santa Barbara, 1983.

BOCKEMÖHL, LEONORE, *Odontoglossum. A Monograph and Iconograph*, Brücke Verlag, Kurt Schmersw., 1989.

COMBER, J.B., *Orchids of Java*, Bentham-Moxon Trust, Royal Botanic Gardens Kew, 1990.

DAKKUS, P.M.W., *Beschrijving van orchideeën die in Nederlands Indië gekweekt worden*, Nix-Bandoeng, Dutch East Indies, 1930.

DUSEK, JINDRA, KRISTEK, JAROSLAV, *Orchideje*, Academia, Prague, 1986.

HILLERMAN & HOLST, *Cultivated Angraecoid orchids of Madagascar*, Timber Press, USA, 1986.

Index periodicarum orchidacearum, 1975—1985, Édition Charles F. Oertle, Switzerland, 1987.

LANCASTER, ROY, *Travels in China*, Antique Collectors' Club Ltd, Woodbridge, 1989.

LECOUFLE, MARCEL, *Orchidées exotiques*, La Maison Rustique, 1981.

LIN TSAN-PIAO, *Native orchids of Taiwan*, National Taiwan University, ROC Taiwan, 1975.

NORTHEN, REBECCA, *Home Orchid Growing*, Nostrand Reinhold, New York, 1970.

PAUL, MICHEL, *Orchids*, Merlin Press, London, 1963.

PAUL, MICHEL, *Orchideeën, zelf kweken en verzorgen in kamer, kas en tuin*, Zomer en Keuning, Wageningen, 1977.

PAUL, MICHEL, *Orchideeën*, C.A.J. van Dishoeck, Bussum, 1963.

PAUL, MICHEL, *Orchideeën in kleur*, Zuidgroep BV, Uitgevers, Den Haag, 1985.

PODEWIJN, DIRK, *Bibliographie Charles Vuylsteke Sr. & Jr., 1867-1937*, Werkcomité Herdenking Charles Vuylsteke, Belgium, 1995.

Proceedings of the 6th World Orchid Conference, 1969, Sydney, 1971.

RITTERSHAUSEN, BRIAN & WILMA, *Orchid Growing Illustrated*, Blandford Press, Poole, 1985.

Sander's List of Orchid Hybrids, 1895–1995, Sander's & Sons, St. Albans and RHS, Vincent Square, London.

SCHWEINFURTH, CHARLES, *Orchids of Peru*, Fieldiana Botany, Natural History Museum, Chicago, 1958-1961.

THOMSON, J., *Proceedings of the 14th World Orchid Conference, 1993*, Glasgow, 1994.

WILLIAMS BRIAN & KRAMER JACK, *Les Orchidées*, Solar, 1983.

WILLIAMS, JOHN G., WILLIAM, ANDREW E. & ARLOTT, NORMAN, *Guide des orchidées sauvages*, Delachaux et Niestlé, 1988.

WITHNER, CARL L., *The Orchids, a Scientific Survey*, The Ronald Press Company, New York, 1959.

Reviews and journals

Brenesia revista de ciencias naturales, no. 37, March 1992, Museo National de Costa Rica San José, Costa Rica.

Malayan Orchid Review, Ossea, PO Box 2363, Singapore 9043.

Orchid Digest, c/o Robert H. Schuler, PO Box 1216, Redlands, 93272-0402, California, USA.

L'orchidée, F.F.A.O., Dr. P.C. Martin, 159 ter, rue de Paris, 95689 Montlignon, France.

Orchideen, Deutsche Orchideen-Gesellschaft, Manfred Wolff, Bahnhofstrasse 24a, D 63533, Mainhausen, Germany.

L'orchidophile, S.F.O., 84, rue de Grenelle, 75007 Paris, France.

The Orchid Review, RHS, 21B Chudleigh Road, Kingsteighton, Newton Abbot, Devon, TQ12 3JT , UK.

Orchids AOS Bulletin, American Orchid Society, Inc, 6000 South Olive Avenue, West Palm Beach, Florida 33405, USA.

Orchids Australia, PO Box 145, Findon, S.A. 5089, Australia.

South African Orchid Journal, PO Box 81, Constantia 7848, South Africa.

Index

Page numbers refer to text or captions, except those in italics,
which indicate illustrations

Societies and associations

Orchid Society of Great Britain, contact:
Mrs. B. Arnold, Athelney, 145 Binscombe Village, Godalming, Surrey, GU7 3QL, UK

Club des orchidophiles wallons, 25 Chassé Isabeau, 7334 Hautrage, Belgium

Jury d'orchidées français, 30 rue Rouget de l'Isle, 95390 Saint Prix, France

Les orchidophiles réunis, 150 rue Vanderborght, 1090 Brussels, Belgium

Société française d'orchidophilie, 84 rue de Grenelle, 75005 Paris, France

Fédération française des amateurs d'orchidées, 159 ter, rue de Paris, 95680 Montlignon, France

Association française de protection d'orchidées, 5 rue Charles Bernard, 94420 Villeneuve-le-Roy, France

Société suisse d'orchidophilie, groupe de Romandie, 37 rue Jean Achard, 1231 Conches, Switzerland

Contents

Acknowledgements

Most of the photographs in this book were taken in the glasshouses of Paul Orchideeën,
Oosteinderweg 129 c, 1432 Aalsmeer, Holland.

The photographer would like to thank orchid-lover Marcel Dumets
for the plants so kindly placed at his disposal.

EVERGREEN is an imprint of Benedikt Taschen Verlag GmbH

© for this edition: 1998 Benedikt Taschen Verlag GmbH
Hohenzollernring 53, D–50672 Köln
© 1997 Editions du Chêne – Hachette Livre – Orchidées
Under the direction of Paul Starosta
Editor: Philippe Pierrelée
Text: Michel Paul
Photographs: Paul Starosta
Cover: Angelika Taschen, Cologne
Translated by Elaine Richards
In association with First Edition Translations Ltd, Cambridge
Realization of the English edition by First Edition Translations Ltd, Cambridge

Printed in Italy
ISBN 3-8228-7762-X